KWELLE PREP

COMMON CORE

GRADE 5

ENGLISH LANGUAGE ARTS

Kweller Prep

Developed by a lawyer, Kweller Prep is an established supplemental education service with a 15-year track record of success in preparing students for specialized middle-school, high-school, college entrance, and graduate school exams. With thousands of acceptances to date, Kweller Prep has built a time-tested learning program with unsurpassed performance. Our competitive advantage is the way in which we operate; we focus on each child individually to ensure success.

Our rigorous program is designed for ambitious students to help them achieve their academic goals. Tutoring centers in Queens and Manhattan serve as learning incubators where parents, students, teachers, tutors, and counselors alike can learn from one another and grow. Nearly every tutor at Kweller Prep is the first one in his or her family to attend a Specialized High School or Top University on a scholarship.

Kweller Prep was created by the vision of Frances Kweller, attorney at law. She was the first one in her immediate family to attend both a top university (New York University - Steinhardt School of Education) and Graduate Program (Juris Doctorate - Hofstra University School of Law). In short, Kweller Prep is designed to help get you where you want to go! 2 locations! Forest Hills, Queens and midtown Manhattan.

Email : info@kwellerprep.com

Website: **www.KwellerPrep.com**

First Edition January 2019.

This is the first edition so if you find any errors, please correct the error and then take a picture of the correction and the page number. Please email it to info@kwellerprep.com. Ms. Kweller will you $1 for any typo you find before May 1, 2019.

TEST PREP TIPS

First of all, remind your student to attention in class throughout the year, g questions as needed on homework classwork. The Language Arts curriculum d follow the exact standards and skills that e tested on the end-of-year assessment.

One of the best ways to prepare for a ng test is by—of course—reading. In the hs leading up to the test, have your student a certain amount of pages or minutes ly from a book that she enjoys. Reading istently will improve your student's reading prehension and enhance her vocabulary, skills that are crucial to success on exam.

Another extremely effective strategy is to tice, practice, practice. Have your student on practice questions and complete at ral full length practice tests. Our practice are a great place to start.

However, simply answering the questions then moving on will not yield much rovement. If your student misses a tion, discuss why the correct answer ndeed correct. Come up with alternate roaches to this question type that may better in the future. Have your student ain her answer to each question. This s you the opportunity to reinforce logical king and correct misconceptions as needed. , it's good practice for finding evidence to port a claim, perhaps the key skill on ELA ing assessments.

Prior to the test, encourage students to a solid night of sleep and eat a nourishing kfast.

For children, avoiding test anxiety is very ortant, so be sure to avoid over-emphasizing

the test or inadvertently causing your student to feel excessive stress or pressure.

In addition, **teach your student general test-taking strategies such as the following:**

Narrow down your answer choices by using process of elimination. This involves crossing out obviously wrong answers to increase your chances of finding the correct answer.

If you get stuck on a question, skip it and come back to it after answering easier questions.

Remember that no one is expected to answer every single correction correctly. Don't panic when you get stuck on a question. Take a deep breath and remember that you are intelligent and prepared.

If you follow the advice here, your student should be well on her way to a stress-free and successful performance on this important assessment.

TABLE OF CONTENTS

Introduction **4**
How To Use This Book **5**
Test Prep Tips **6**

Reading: Literature **7**
Supporting Statements (RL.5.1) 8
Determine Theme & Summarize Text (RL.5.2) 13
Compare and Contrast Two or More Characters, Settings, or Events (RL.5.3) 19
Determine Word Meaning in Text, Including Figurative Language (RL.5.4) 25
Organization (RL.5.5) 28
Describe How Point of View Influences Events (RL.5.6) 33
Analyze How Images Contribute to Text (RL.5.7) 37
Compare & Contrast Stories in Same Genre (RL.5.9) 41

Reading: Information **45**
Quote Accurately and Draw Inferences from a Text (RI.5.1) 46
Determine Main Idea and Summarize Text (RI.5.2) 51
Explain Relationships Between Individuals, Events, and Ideas in Texts (RI.5.3) 56
Determine Academic and Domain-Specific Word Meaning in Text (RI.5.4) 60
Compare & Contrast Structure of Events, Ideas or Information in Texts (RI.5.5) 64
Analyze & Compare/Contrast Multiple Accounts of Same Topic (RI.5.6) 68
Explain How Authors Use Evidence to Support Points of View (RI.5.8) 71
Integrate & Explain Information from Several Texts (RI.5.9) 75

Language **79**
Have Command of Grammar & Usage (L.5.1) 80
Know Capitalization, Punctuation & Spelling (L.5.2) 84
Understand & Use Appropriate Language Conventions (L.5.3) 88
Determine Meaning of Unknown Words When Reading (L.5.4) 91
Understand Figurative Language and Word Relationships (L.5.5) 96
Know & Use General Academic/Domain-Specific Words (L.5.6) 100

Answer Key and Explanations **105**

Practice Tests **123**
Practice Test One and Answer Explanations 125
Practice Test Two and Answer Explanations 163

INTRODUCTION

Common Core Standards/ Next Generation Learning Standards

States all across the USA have implemented rigorous standards called the "Common Core Standards."

These standards, or learning goals, outline what students in each grade should learn each year. They emphasize just how important the new goals are: they can help show whether students are on the right track to college and beyond, even when the students are years from those life stages.

In 2018, NY introduced the "Next Generation Learning Standards", which are very similar to the Common Core standards in that they also focus on higher level critical thinking skills, problem solving, analysis, and real-world application.

NY State English Language Arts (ELA) Assessments

The NY State ELA assessment is designed to determine whether students have mastered grade level appropriate reading, writing and language skills. The ELA assessment is given annually in grades 3-8, and is administered in either computer-based or paper-based format.

The test is divided into two sessions ('Reading' and 'Writing') that are administered over two days. Students will be provided as much time as necessary to complete each test session.

On average, students in Grades 3–4 will likely need approximately 60–70 minutes of working time to complete each of the two test sessions. Students in Grades 5–8 will likely need approximately 80–90 minutes of working time to complete each of the two test sessions.

Question Format on NY State ELA Assessments

All questions will be based on close reading of informational and literary texts, including paired texts. There are three major question formats on NY State ELA exams.

Multiple-Choice Questions: For multiple-choice questions, students select the correct response from four answer choices. These questions ask students to analyze different aspects of a given text, including central idea, style elements, character and plot development, and vocabulary. Reading and Language Standards will be assessed using multiple-choice questions.

Short-Response Questions: These are single questions which ask the student to make an inference (a claim, position, or conclusion) based on his or her analysis of the passage, and then provide two pieces of text-based evidence to support his or her answer. In responding to these questions, students are expected to write in complete sentences. Responses require no more than three complete sentences. Short-response questions will primarily assess reading, but will also require writing and command of language.

Extended-Response Questions: Extended-response questions are essay questions designed to measure a student's ability to write from sources, and prompt students to communicate a clear and coherent analysis of one or two texts.

HOW TO USE THIS BOOK

The objective of this book is to provide students, educators, and parents with practice materials focused on the core skills needed to help students succeed on the NY ELA reading assessment.

A student will fare better on an assessment when s/he has practiced and mastered the skills measured by the test. A student also excels when s/he is familiar with the format and structure of the test. This book helps students do both. Students can review key material by standard through doing the skill-building exercises, as well as take practice tests to become accustomed to how the content is presented and to enhance test-taking skills. By test day, students will feel confident and be adequately prepared to do his or her best.

This Book Includes:

- 196 Skill building exercises organised by standard in order to help students learn and review concepts in the order that they will likely be presented in the classroom. These worksheets also help identify weaknesses, and highlight and strengthen the skills needed to excel on the actual exam. A variety of question types are included in the worksheets to help students build skills in answering questions in multiple formats, and to help students stay engaged while they work through problems.

- Our ELA practice tests are based on the official NY ELA assessments released by the test administrator. Our practice tests include similar question types and the same rigorous content found on the official assessments. By using these materials, students will become familiar with the types of items (including

Technology Enhanced presented in a paper response formats they test. Two practice test the end of the book.

pay ask and sho will

- Answer keys with deta to help students not m mistakes again. These clear up common misc indicate how students answer to a question.

rea mo rea wee con con two the

- The answer explanatio practice tests also iden that the question is ass student is having diffic encourage the student area by practicing the in the workbook.

pra wo sev tes

- Test prep tips to help st the test strategically an

and im qu qu is ap wo ex gi th Pl su re

ge br

im

TABLE OF CONTENTS

Introduction 4

How To Use This Book 5

Test Prep Tips 6

Reading: Literature 7

Supporting Statements (RL.5.1) 8

Determine Theme & Summarize Text (RL.5.2) 13

Compare and Contrast Two or More Characters, Settings, or Events (RL.5.3) 19

Determine Word Meaning in Text, Including Figurative Language (RL.5.4) 25

Organization (RL.5.5) 28

Describe How Point of View Influences Events (RL.5.6) 33

Analyze How Images Contribute to Text (RL.5.7) 37

Compare & Contrast Stories in Same Genre (RL.5.9) 41

Reading: Information 45

Quote Accurately and Draw Inferences from a Text (RI.5.1) 46

Determine Main Idea and Summarize Text (RI.5.2) 51

Explain Relationships Between Individuals, Events, and Ideas in Texts (RI.5.3) 56

Determine Academic and Domain-Specific Word Meaning in Text (RI.5.4) 60

Compare & Contrast Structure of Events, Ideas or Information in Texts (RI.5.5) 64

Analyze & Compare/Contrast Multiple Accounts of Same Topic (RI.5.6) 68

Explain How Authors Use Evidence to Support Points of View (RI.5.8) 71

Integrate & Explain Information from Several Texts (RI.5.9) 75

Language 79

Have Command of Grammar & Usage (L.5.1) 80

Know Capitalization, Punctuation & Spelling (L.5.2) 84

Understand & Use Appropriate Language Conventions (L.5.3) 88

Determine Meaning of Unknown Words When Reading (L.5.4) 91

Understand Figurative Language and Word Relationships (L.5.5) 96

Know & Use General Academic/Domain-Specific Words (L.5.6) ... 100

Answer Key and Explanations 105

Practice Tests 123

Practice Test One and Answer Explanations 125

Practice Test Two and Answer Explanations 163

INTRODUCTION

Common Core Standards/ Next Generation Learning Standards

States all across the USA have implemented rigorous standards called the "Common Core Standards."

These standards, or learning goals, outline what students in each grade should learn each year. They emphasize just how important the new goals are: they can help show whether students are on the right track to college and beyond, even when the students are years from those life stages.

In 2018, NY introduced the "Next Generation Learning Standards", which are very similar to the Common Core standards in that they also focus on higher level critical thinking skills, problem solving, analysis, and real-world application.

NY State English Language Arts (ELA) Assessments

The NY State ELA assessment is designed to determine whether students have mastered grade level appropriate reading,writing and language skills. The ELA assessment is given annually in grades 3-8, and is administered in either computer-based or paper-based format.

The test is divided into two sessions ('Reading' and 'Writing') that are administered over two days. Students will be provided as much time as necessary to complete each test session.

On average, students in Grades 3–4 will likely need approximately 60–70 minutes of working time to complete each of the two test sessions. Students in Grades 5-8 will likely need approximately 80–90 minutes of working time to complete each of the two test sessions.

Question Format on NY State ELA Assessments

All questions will be based on close reading of informational and literary texts, including paired texts. There are three major question formats on NY State ELA exams.

Multiple-Choice Questions: For multiple-choice questions, students select the correct response from four answer choices. These questions ask students to analyze different aspects of a given text, including central idea, style elements, character and plot development, and vocabulary. Reading and Language Standards will be assessed using multiple-choice questions.

Short-Response Questions: These are single questions which ask the student to make an inference (a claim, position, or conclusion) based on his or her analysis of the passage, and then provide two pieces of text-based evidence to support his or her answer. In responding to these questions, students are expected to write in complete sentences. Responses require no more than three complete sentences. Short-response questions will primarily assess reading, but will also require writing and command of language.

Extended-Response Questions: Extended-response questions are essay questions designed to measure a student's ability to write from sources, and prompt students to communicate a clear and coherent analysis of one or two texts.

HOW TO USE THIS BOOK

The objective of this book is to provide students, educators, and parents with practice materials focused on the core skills needed to help students succeed on the NY ELA reading assessment.

A student will fare better on an assessment when s/he has practiced and mastered the skills measured by the test. A student also excels when s/he is familiar with the format and structure of the test. This book helps students do both. Students can review key material by standard through doing the skill-building exercises, as well as take practice tests to become accustomed to how the content is presented and to enhance test-taking skills. By test day, students will feel confident and be adequately prepared to do his or her best.

This Book Includes:

- 196 Skill building exercises organised by standard in order to help students learn and review concepts in the order that they will likely be presented in the classroom. These worksheets also help identify weaknesses, and highlight and strengthen the skills needed to excel on the actual exam. A variety of question types are included in the worksheets to help students build skills in answering questions in multiple formats, and to help students stay engaged while they work through problems.

- Our ELA practice tests are based on the official NY ELA assessments released by the test administrator. Our practice tests include similar question types and the same rigorous content found on the official assessments. By using these materials, students will become familiar with the types of items (including

Technology Enhanced Items (TEIs) presented in a paper based format) and response formats they may see on the test. Two practice tests are included at the end of the book.

- Answer keys with detailed explanations to help students not make the same mistakes again. These explanations help clear up common misconceptions and indicate how students might arrive at an answer to a question.

- The answer explanations for the practice tests also identify the standard/s that the question is assessing. If a student is having difficulty in one area, encourage the student to improve in that area by practicing the specific set of skills in the workbook.

- Test prep tips to help students approach the test strategically and with confidence.

TEST PREP TIPS

First of all, remind your student to pay attention in class throughout the year, asking questions as needed on homework and classwork. The Language Arts curriculum should follow the exact standards and skills that will be tested on the end-of-year assessment.

One of the best ways to prepare for a reading test is by—of course—reading. In the months leading up to the test, have your student read a certain amount of pages or minutes weekly from a book that she enjoys. Reading consistently will improve your student's reading comprehension and enhance her vocabulary, two skills that are crucial to success on the exam.

Another extremely effective strategy is to practice, practice, practice. Have your student work on practice questions and complete at several full length practice tests. Our practice tests are a great place to start.

However, simply answering the questions and then moving on will not yield much improvement. If your student misses a question, discuss why the correct answer is indeed correct. Come up with alternate approaches to this question type that may work better in the future. Have your student explain her answer to each question. This gives you the opportunity to reinforce logical thinking and correct misconceptions as needed. Plus, it's good practice for finding evidence to support a claim, perhaps the key skill on ELA reading assessments.

Prior to the test, encourage students to get a solid night of sleep and eat a nourishing breakfast.

For children, avoiding test anxiety is very important, so be sure to avoid over-emphasizing the test or inadvertently causing your student to feel excessive stress or pressure.

In addition, **teach your student general test-taking strategies such as the following:**

Narrow down your answer choices by using process of elimination. This involves crossing out obviously wrong answers to increase your chances of finding the correct answer.

If you get stuck on a question, skip it and come back to it after answering easier questions.

Remember that no one is expected to answer every single correction correctly. Don't panic when you get stuck on a question. Take a deep breath and remember that you are intelligent and prepared.

If you follow the advice here, your student should be well on her way to a stress-free and successful performance on this important assessment.

READING: LITERATURE

SUPPORTING STATEMENTS

RL.5.1: Quote accurately from a text when explaining what the text says explicitly and when drawing inferences from the text.

Directions: Read the passage and answer the questions that follow.

Passage 1: Excerpt from *The Wizard of Oz*
by L. Frank Baum

1   The train from 'Frisco was very late. It should have arrived at Hugson's Siding at midnight, but it was already five o'clock and the gray dawn was breaking in the east when the little train slowly rumbled up to the open shed that served for the station-house. As it came to a stop the conductor called out in a loud voice:

2   "Hugson's Siding!"

3   At once a little girl rose from her seat and walked to the door of the car, carrying a wicker suit-case in one hand and a round bird-cage covered up with newspapers in the other, while a parasol was tucked under her arm. The conductor helped her off the car and then the engineer started his train again, so that it puffed and groaned and moved slowly away up the track. The reason he was so late was because all through the night there were times when the solid earth shook and trembled under him, and the engineer was afraid that at any moment the rails might spread apart and an accident happen to his passengers. So he moved the cars slowly and with caution.

4   The little girl stood still to watch until the train had disappeared around a curve; then she turned to see where she was.

5   The shed at Hugson's Siding was bare save for an old wooden bench, and did not look very inviting. As she peered through the soft gray light not a house of any sort was visible near the station, nor was any person in sight; but after a while the child discovered a horse and buggy standing near a group of trees a short distance away. She walked toward it and found the horse tied to a tree and standing motionless, with its head hanging down almost to the ground. It was a big horse, tall and bony, with long legs and large knees and feet. She could count his ribs easily where they showed through the skin of his body, and his head was long and seemed altogether too big for him, as if it did not fit. His tail was short and scraggly, and his harness had been broken in many places and fastened together again with cords and bits of wire. The buggy seemed almost new, for it had a shiny top and side curtains. Getting around in front, so that she could look inside, the girl saw a boy curled up on the seat, fast asleep.

6   She set down the bird-cage and poked the boy with her parasol. Presently he woke up, rose to a sitting position and rubbed his eyes briskly.

7 "Hello!" he said, seeing her, "are you Dorothy Gale?"

8 "Yes," she answered, looking gravely at his tousled hair and blinking gray eyes. "Have you come to take me to Hugson's Ranch?"

9 "Of course," he answered. "Train in?"

10 "I couldn't be here if it wasn't," she said.

11 He laughed at that, and his laugh was merry and frank. Jumping out of the buggy he put Dorothy's suit-case under the seat and her bird-cage on the floor in front.

12 "Canary-birds?" he asked.

13 "Oh, no; it's just Eureka, my kitten. I thought that was the best way to carry her."

14 The boy nodded.

15 "Eureka's a funny name for a cat," he remarked.

16 "I named my kitten that because I found it," she explained. "Uncle Henry says 'Eureka' means 'I have found it.'"

1. The following question has two parts. First, answer Part A and then Part B.

Part A
Why did the train not arrive on time?

    A. The train was late because the rails were made of unsafe materials.

    B. The engineer had become sick and nearly passed out making the train shake uncontrollably.

    C. The train was late because there was an earthquake.

    D. The train was re-routed to avoid a severe storm.

Part B
Which detail from the passage supports the answer to Part A?

    A. "...the little train slowly rumbled up to the open shed that served for the station-house." (paragraph 1)

    B. "...it puffed and groaned and moved slowly away up the track."(paragraph 3)

    C. "It should have arrived at Hugson's siding at midnight."(paragraph 1)

    D. "all through the night there were times when the solid earth shook and trembled under him." (paragraph 3)

2. Where was the little girl's destination?
    A. her cousin Eugene's house
    B. Hugson's Ranch
    C. 'Frisco
    D. Hugson's Siding

3. How long has the boy been waiting for the little girl?
    A. He had been waiting so long, he had fallen asleep.
    B. He had just pulled in minutes before her.
    C. He was not there when she arrived, and she had to watch the train drive off wondering if she would be stuck at the station all alone.
    D. They arrived at the same time.

4. The following question has two parts. First, answer Part A and then Part B.

Part A
How does the little girl respond to the boy's question, "Train In?"(paragraph 9)
    A. She tells him the train did not arrive yet.
    B. She shows him that his question is silly and does not make sense.
    C. She makes him start to cry.
    D. She asks if he likes cats.

Part B
Which detail from the passage supports the answer to Part A?
    A. "The train from 'Frisco was very late. " (paragraph 1)
    B. "...his laugh was merry and frank." (paragraph 11)
    C. ""Have you come to take me to Hugson's Ranch?'" (paragraph 13)
    D. ""I couldn't be here if it wasn't," she said."(paragraph 10)

5. The following question has two parts. First, answer Part A and then Part B.

Part A
Why does Dorothy-Gale have a bird cage?
    A. She has birds with her.
    B. There are bird waiting for her at her destination.
    C. She is transporting her cat.
    D. She is using it to carry her supplies.

Part B

Which detail from the passage supports the answer to Part A?

    A. "…he put Dorothy's suit-case under the seat and her bird-cage on the floor in front."(paragraph 11)

    B. " "Oh, no; it's just Eureka, my kitten. I thought that was the best way to carry her.""(paragraph 13)

    C. " "Canary-birds?" he asked."(paragraph 12)

    D. " "Eureka's a funny name for a cat," he remarked."(paragraph 15)

6. What observation does the girl make about the boy's transportation?

    A. The buggy is in need of being replaced.

    B. The horse seems too weak to pull the buggy.

    C. The buggy is in much nicer condition than the horse and its harness.

    D. The harness is broken making it impossible to connect the horse to the buggy.

7. Based on the details from the passage, what does Dorothy-Ann think about the boy?

_____

_____

_____

_____

_____

_____

_____

8. Based on the details from the passage, who is Eureka, and how did she get her name?

_____

_____

_____

_____

_____

_____

_____

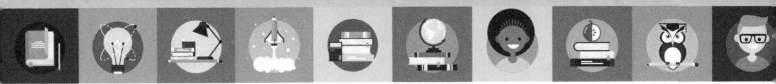

9. Is Dorothy-Ann observant? Provide at least two pieces of evidence from the text to support your answer.

_____

_____

_____

_____

_____

_____

_____

_____

_____

DETERMINE THEME & SUMMARIZE TEXT

RL.5.2 Determine a theme of a story, drama, or poem from details in the text, including how characters in a story or drama respond to challenges or how the speaker in a poem reflects upon a topic; summarize the text.

Directions: Read the passage and answer the questions below.

Passage 2: "Icarus and Daedalus"
by Josephine Preston Peabody

1   Among all those mortals who grew so wise that they learned the secrets of the gods, none was more cunning than Daedalus.

2   He once built, for King Minos of Crete, a wonderful Labyrinth of winding ways so cunningly tangled up and twisted around that, once inside, you could never find your way out again without a magic clue. But the king's favor veered with the wind, and one day he had his master architect imprisoned in a tower. Daedalus managed to escape from his cell; but it seemed impossible to leave the island, since every ship that came or went was well guarded by order of the king.

3   At length, watching the sea-gulls in the air—the only creatures that were sure of liberty—he thought of a plan for himself and his young son Icarus, who was captive with him.

4   Little by little, he gathered a store of feathers great and small. He fastened these together with thread, molded them in with wax, and so fashioned two great wings like those of a bird. When they were done, Daedalus fitted them to his own shoulders, and after one or two efforts, he found that by waving his arms he could winnow the air and cleave it, as a swimmer does the sea. He held himself aloft, wavered this way and that with the wind, and at last, like a great fledgling, he learned to fly.

5   Without delay, he fell to work on a pair of wings for the boy Icarus, and taught him carefully how to use them, bidding him beware of rash adventures among the stars. "Remember," said the father, "never to fly very low or very high, for the fogs about the earth would weigh you down, but the blaze of the sun will surely melt your feathers apart if you go too near."

6   For Icarus, these cautions went in at one ear and out by the other. Who could remember to be careful when he was to fly for the first time? Are birds careful? Not they! And not an idea remained in the boy's head but the one joy of escape.

7   The day came, and the fair wind that was to set them free. The father put on his wings, and, while the light urged them to be gone, he waited to see that all was well with Icarus, for the two could not fly hand in hand. Up they rose, the boy after his father. The hateful ground of Crete sank beneath them; and the country folk, who caught a glimpse of them when they were high above the tree-tops, took it for a vision of the gods—Apollo, perhaps—with Cupid after him.

8   At first there was a terror in the joy. The wide vacancy of the air dazed them—a glance downward made their brains reel. But when a great wind filled their wings, and Icarus felt himself sustained, like a halcyon-bird in the hollow of a wave, like a child uplifted by his mother, he forgot everything in the world but joy. He forgot Crete and the other islands that he had passed over: he saw but vaguely that winged thing in the distance before him that was his father Daedalus. He longed for one draught of flight to quench the thirst of his captivity: he stretched out his arms to the sky and made towards the highest heavens.

9   Alas for him! Warmer and warmer grew the air. Those arms, that had seemed to uphold him, relaxed. His wings wavered, drooped. He fluttered his young hands vainly—he was falling—and in that terror he remembered. The heat of the sun had melted the wax from his wings; the feathers were falling, one by one, like snowflakes; and there was none to help.

10 He fell like a leaf tossed down the wind, down, down, with one cry that overtook Daedalus far away. When Daedalus returned, and sought high and low for the poor boy, he saw nothing but the bird-like feathers afloat on the water, and he knew that Icarus was drowned.

11 The nearest island he named Icaria, in memory of the child; but he, in heavy grief, went to the temple of Apollo in Sicily, and there hung up his wings as an offering. Never again did he attempt to fly.

1. This question has two parts. First, answer Part A. Then, answer Part B.

Part A
Which of the following statements BEST reflects the theme of Passage 1?

    A. It's better to be a captive in safety than put your family in danger for freedom.

    B. We should listen to the warnings that are given for our safety.

    C. Adventure is a dangerous pursuit.

    D. Humanity was never meant to fly.

Part B

Which quote from the text best supports your answer in Part A?

    A. "At length, watching the sea-gulls in the air—the only creatures that were sure of liberty—he thought of a plan for himself and his young son Icarus, who was captive with him." (Paragraph 3)

    B. "He held himself aloft, wavered this way and that with the wind, and at last, like a great fledgling, he learned to fly." (Paragraph 4)

    C. "'Remember,' said the father, 'never to fly very low or very high, for the fogs about the earth would weigh you down, but the blaze of the sun will surely melt your feathers apart if you go too near.'" (Paragraph 5)

    D. "Never again did he attempt to fly." (Paragraph 11)

2. Which of the following is NOT a conflict Daedalus faced in Passage 1?

    A. being in prison

    B. power of the gods

    C. a son's disobedience

    D. the laws of nature

3. Which of the following is the BEST summary of Passage 1?

    A. King Minos put Daedalus in prison, but he found a way to escape.

    B. Daedalus learned how to fly but ended up losing his son in the process.

    C. Icarus learned how to fly with his father Daedalus, but failed to heed his father's warnings and crashed into the ocean.

    D. Daedalus refused to fly ever again after losing his son to the ocean.

4. A possible secondary theme of the story is that people sometimes abuse their power toward those with less power. Which of the following quotes supports this idea?

    A. "But the king's favor veered with the wind, and one day he had his master architect imprisoned in a tower." (Paragraph 1)

    B. "'Remember,' said the father, 'never to fly very low or very high, for the fogs about the earth would weigh you down, but the blaze of the sun will surely melt your feathers apart if you go too near.'" (Paragraph 5)

    C. "He longed for one draught of flight to quench the thirst of his captivity: he stretched out his arms to the sky and made towards the highest heavens." (Paragraph 8)

    D. "The nearest island he named Icaria, in memory of the child; but he, in heavy grief, went to the temple of Apollo in Sicily, and there hung up his wings as an offering. Never again did he attempt to fly." (Paragraph 11)

Passage 2: The Story of the Lazy Boy

1   There was once a very lazy boy. And when everybody else had planted out his paddy, he was only setting forth to plough. But the old man of the season, seeing him, said, "The season has gone; what are you ploughing for now? The paddy is all planted out, and it is late."

2   But the boy would not listen to him, and ploughed sturdily ahead, beating his cattle soundly as he went. And when the old man again and again questioned him, he cried, "What sort of old man is this? Can he not see that I am busy? I know very well what I am about."

3   But the old man said gently, "Nay, my son: but it is for your good that I would speak to you."

4   And the boy said, "Speak quickly then, and have done with it."

5   And the old man said, "My son, the season is gone; what avails it to plough now?"

6   And then the boy cried, "Where has it gone? And when has it gone? And why has it gone? And how shall I find it?"

7   But the old man of the season said, "You should have ploughed when others did. The season has gone, and no man can bring it back."

8   But the boy said, "I must bring it back; else, how shall I eat, and how shall I live? Do tell me where it is gone."

9   And as he would not let the god go, finally, losing patience, the old man said, "You go over there, and you will find an old man with a snow-white head ploughing in a field. You get hold of him and do as he tells you." So saying, the old man made his escape. Then the lad hastened home to his mother and bade her cook supper quickly, and tie him up some rice to take with him on the morrow, for he was going to bring back the departed season for ploughing.

10   "For," said he, "when I was ploughing to-day, an old man told me that the season was gone, and that if I went after him and pursued him I would find him, and that I must do as he would tell me." So his mother rose very early in the morning, and, giving him something to eat and drink, sent him on his way.

11   And as he went, he asked all he met, "Can you tell me where the old man of the season has gone?"

12   But they said, "Everyone knows that the season is gone, but where it is gone, or why it is gone, who can say?"

13 At last, when he was nearly in despair, he saw an old man ploughing afar off, and shouted to him, "Stay a moment, father, stay; I want to ask you a question."

14 But the old man was busy, and went his way. Then the lad pursued him and never ceased calling after him till at last the old man losing patience, turned upon him, and said, "What pertinacious noisy lad is this, who won't leave me alone?"

15 But the lad said, "Be not angry, my father; I am fallen into great trouble, and it behooves you to help me."

16 "Speak quickly, then," said the old man.

17 And the boy said, "I take you to be the old man of the season, and I pray you not to slay me. All the others have planted out their paddy, and I have fallen behind, and have planted nothing."

18 But the old man said, "It is too late for me to return. Go you back, and plant your paddy as best you can." And so the lad hastened back and planted out his seedlings in such heedless haste as became him. And that's all.

5. This question has two parts. First, answer Part A. Then, answer Part B.

Part A
Which of the following statements BEST reflects the theme of Passage 2?
- **A.** It's never too late to begin working hard.
- **B.** Laziness fades with age.
- **C.** There's always reason to hope when working hard.
- **D.** No matter how hard you work, you can't make up for lost time.

Part B
Which quote from the text best supports your answer in Part A?
- **A.** "But the boy would not listen to him, and ploughed sturdily ahead, beating his cattle soundly as he went." (Paragraph 2)
- **B.** "And then the boy cried, 'Where has it gone? And when has it gone? And why has it gone? And how shall I find it?'" (Paragraph 6)
- **C.** "But the old man of the season said, 'You should have ploughed when others did. The season has gone, and no man can bring it back.'" (Paragraph 7)
- **D.** "At last, when he was nearly in despair, he saw an old man ploughing afar off, and shouted to him, 'Stay a moment, father, stay; I want to ask you a question.'" (Paragraph 13)

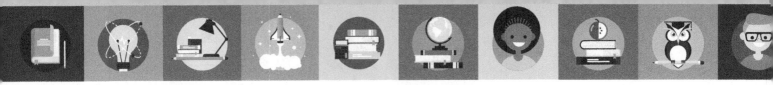

6. How are Passage 1 and Passage 2 thematically similar? Use details from the texts to support your response.

_____

_____

_____

_____

_____

7. What was the main conflict in Passage 2?
   A. the boy and his paddy
   B. the boy and his laziness
   C. the boy and the old men
   D. the boy and his mother

8. Summarize Passage 2 in your own words.

_____

_____

_____

_____

_____

COMPARE & CONTRAST CHARACTERS, SETTINGS OR EVENTS

RL.5.3: Compare and contrast two or more characters, settings, or events in a story or drama, drawing on specific details in the text (e.g., how characters interact).

Directions: Read the passage and answer the questions that follow.

Passage 1: Excerpt from *Raggedy Ann Stories:* "Raggedy Ann Learns a Lesson"
by Johnny Gruelle

1   One day the dolls were left all to themselves.

2   Their little mistress had placed them all around the room and told them to be nice children while she was away.

3   There they sat and never even so much as wiggled a finger, until their mistress had left the room.

4   When the front gate clicked and the dolls knew they were alone in the house, they all scrambled to their feet.

5   "Now let's have a good time!" cried the tin soldier. "Let's all go in search of something to eat!"

6   "Yes! Let's all go in search of something to eat!" cried all the other dolls.

7   "When Mistress had me out playing with her this morning," said Raggedy Ann, "she carried me by a door near the back of the house and I smelled something which smelled as if it would taste delicious!"

8   "Then you lead the way, Raggedy Ann!" cried the French doll.

9   "I think it would be a good plan to elect Raggedy Ann as our leader on this expedition!" said the Indian doll.

10   At this all the other dolls clapped their hands together and shouted, "Hurrah! Raggedy Ann will be our leader."

11   "Follow me!" she cried as her wobbly legs carried her across the floor at a lively pace.

12   The other dolls followed, racing about the house until they came to the pantry door. "This is the place!" cried Raggedy Ann, and sure enough, all the dolls smelled something which they knew must be very good to eat. But none of the dolls was tall enough to open the door.

READING: LITERATURE

13 The dolls were talking and pulling and pushing and every once in a while one would fall over and the others would step on her in their efforts to open the door. Finally Raggedy Ann drew away from the others and sat down on the floor.

14 When the other dolls discovered Raggedy Ann sitting there, running her rag hands through her yarn hair, they knew she was thinking.

15 "Sh! Sh!" they said to each other and quietly went over near Raggedy Ann and sat down in front of her.

16 "There must be a way to get inside," said Raggedy Ann.

17 "I can't seem to think clearly today," said Raggedy Ann. "It feels as if my head were ripped."

18 At this the French doll ran to Raggedy Ann and took off her bonnet. "Yes, there is a rip in your head, Raggedy!" she said and pulled a pin from her skirt and pinned up Raggedy's head. "It's not a very neat job, for I got some puckers in it!" she said.

19 "Oh that is ever so much better!" cried Raggedy Ann. "Now I can think quite clearly."

20 "Now Raggedy can think quite clearly!" cried all the dolls.

21 "My thoughts must have leaked out the rip before!" said Raggedy Ann.

22 "Now that I can think so clearly," said Raggedy Ann, "I think the door must be locked and to get in we must unlock it!"

23 "That will be easy!" said the Dutch doll, "For we will have the brave tin soldier shoot the key out of the lock!"

24 "I can easily do that!" cried the tin soldier, as he raised his gun.

25 "Oh, Raggedy Ann!" cried the French doll. "Please do not let him shoot!"

26 "No!" said Raggedy Ann. "We must think of a quieter way!"

27 After thinking quite hard for a moment, Raggedy Ann jumped up and said: "I have it!" And she caught up the Jumping Jack and held him up to the door; then Jack slid up his stick and unlocked the door.

28 Then the dolls all pushed and the door swung open.

29 My! Such a scramble! The dolls piled over one another in their desire to be the first at the goodies.

1. This question has two parts. First, answer Part A. Then, answer Part B.

Part A: Which doll was the first to speak up about breaking the mistress' rules?
    A. the tin soldier
    B. Raggedy Ann
    C. the Indian doll
    D. Jumping Jack

Part B: Which specific detail from the passage best supports your answer from Part A:
    A. "Now let's have a good time!" cried the tin soldier.
    B. When the front gate clicked and the dolls knew they were alone in the house, they all scrambled to their feet.
    C. "Then you lead the way, Raggedy Ann!" cried the French doll.
    D. "Yes! Let's all go in search of something to eat!" cried all the other dolls.

2. This question has two parts. First, answer Part A. Then, answer Part B.

Part A: Do the other dolls agree with the Indian doll's suggestion about who should be the leader?
    A. No, the French doll wants to be in charge.
    B. No, the tin soldier thinks he should be in charge, since it was his idea.
    C. Yes, the other dolls all think Raggedy Ann should be the leader.
    D. No, the other dolls want the Jumping Jack to be in charge, since he will solve their problem.

Part B: What is a specific detail from the passage that supports your answer from Part A:
    A. "Then you lead the way, Raggedy Ann!" cried the French doll.
    B. "All the other dolls clapped their hands together and shouted, "Hurrah! Raggedy Ann will be our leader."
    C. "Follow me!" she cried as her wobbly legs carried her across the floor at a lively pace.
    D. Finally Raggedy Ann drew away from the others and sat down on the floor.

3. Which word best describes the characters' abilities to get from their room to inside the pantry?
    A. hungry
    B. determined
    C. disobedient
    D. panicked

4. Which detail from the passage best supports that Raggedy Ann was the strongest thinker?

    A. "Yes, there is a rip in your head, Raggedy!" she said and pulled a pin from her skirt and pinned up Raggedy's head.

    B. "This is the place!" cried Raggedy Ann, and sure enough, all the dolls smelled something which they knew must be very good to eat.

    C. "At this the French doll ran to Raggedy Ann and took off her bonnet."

    D. "When the other dolls discovered Raggedy Ann sitting there, running her rag hands through her yarn hair, they knew she was thinking."

Directions: Read the passage and answer the questions that follow.

Passage 2: Excerpt from The Wind in the Willows "The River Bank"
by Kenneth Grahame

1   The Mole had been working very hard all the morning, spring-cleaning his little home. First with brooms, then with dusters; then on ladders and steps and chairs, with a brush and a pail of whitewash; till he had dust in his throat and eyes, and splashes of whitewash all over his black fur, and an aching back and weary arms. Spring was moving in the air above and in the earth below and around him, penetrating even his dark and lowly little house with its spirit of divine discontent and longing. It was small wonder, then, that he suddenly flung down his brush on the floor, said 'Bother!' and 'O blow!' and also 'Hang spring-cleaning!' and bolted out of the house without even waiting to put on his coat. Something up above was calling him, and he made for the steep little tunnel. So he scraped and scratched and scrabbled and scrooged and then he scrooged again and scrabbled and scratched and scraped, working busily with his little paws and muttering to himself, 'Up we go! Up we go!' till at last, pop! his snout came out into the sunlight, and he found himself rolling in the warm grass of a great meadow.

2   'This is fine!' he said to himself. 'This is better than whitewashing!' The sunshine struck hot on his fur, soft breezes caressed his heated brow. Jumping off all his four legs at once, in the joy of living and the delight of spring without its cleaning, he pursued his way across the meadow till he reached the hedge on the further side.

3   It all seemed too good to be true. Hither and thither through the meadows he rambled busily, along the hedgerows, finding everywhere birds building, flowers budding, leaves thrusting—everything happy. And instead of having an uneasy conscience pricking him and whispering 'whitewash!' he somehow could only feel how jolly it was to be the only idle dog among all these busy citizens. After all, the best part of a holiday is perhaps not so much to be resting yourself, as to see all the other fellows busy working.

4   He thought his happiness was complete when, as he meandered aimlessly along, suddenly he stood by the edge of a full-fed river. Never in his life had he seen a river before—this sleek, sinuous, full-bodied animal, chasing and chuckling, gripping things with a gurgle and leaving them with a laugh, to fling itself on fresh playmates that shook themselves free, and were caught and held again. All was a-shake and a-shiver—glints and gleams and sparkles, rustle and swirl, chatter and bubble. The Mole was bewitched, entranced, fascinated. By the side of the river he trotted as one trots, when very small, by the side of a man who holds one spell-bound by exciting stories; and when tired at last, he sat on the bank, while the river still chattered on.

5. This question has two parts. First, answer Part A. Then, answer Part B.

Part A: Where does the Mole live?
  A. close to the river
  B. in the meadow
  C. at the hedge
  D. underground

Part B: What is a specific detail from the passage that supports your answer from part A?
  A. "….he pursued his way across the meadow"….
  B. "….he reached the hedge on the further side."
  C. "….suddenly he stood by the edge of a full-fed river."
  D. "….til at last, pop! his snout came out into the sunlight…."

6. This question has two parts. First, answer Part A. Then, answer Part B.

Part A: What event is occurring based on the animal's' actions throughout the story?
  A. Winter is nearing.
  B. The weather is improving after a snowfall.
  C. Fall has arrived.
  D. Spring has arrived.

Part B: Which details from the passage support your answer from Part A? Check **ALL** that apply.
  ☐ **1** "Spring was moving in the air above…"
  ☐ **2** "After all, the best part of a holiday is perhaps not so much to be resting yourself, as to see all the other fellows busy working."
  ☐ **3** "Hither and thither through the meadows he rambled busily, along the hedgerows, finding everywhere birds building, flowers budding, leaves thrusting…"
  ☐ **4** "…he suddenly flung down his brush on the floor, said 'Bother!'"
  ☐ **5** "…he scraped and scratched and scrabbled and scrooged and then he scrooged again and scrabbled and scratched and scraped…"

READING: LITERATURE

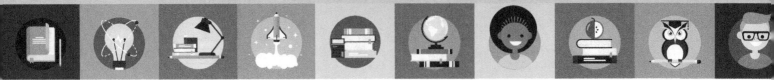

7. How does the Mole's attitude change, as the setting changes? Provide at least **two** details from the passage.

_____

_____

_____

_____

_____

_____

8. Read this excerpt from the passage:

"Never in his life had he seen a river before—this sleek, sinuous, full-bodied animal, chasing and chuckling, gripping things with a gurgle and leaving them with a laugh, to fling itself on fresh playmates that shook themselves free, and were caught and held again. All was a-shake and a-shiver—glints and gleams and sparkles, rustle and swirl, chatter and bubble. The Mole was bewitched, entranced, fascinated. By the side of the river he trotted as one trots, when very small, by the side of a man who holds one spell-bound by exciting stories; and when tired at last, he sat on the bank, while the river still chattered on. "

This excerpt is used mainly to:

    A. show how Mole loves other full-bodied animals
    B. contrast the river's mesmerizing and exciting qualities to Mole compared to Mole's experience of cleaning his underground home
    C. reveal how lazy Mole can be
    D. introduce the new character of a man who tells exciting stories

DETERMINE WORD MEANING IN TEXT, INCLUDING FIGURATIVE LANGUAGE

RL.5.4 Determine the meaning of words and phrases as they are used in a text, including figurative language such as metaphors and similes.

Directions: Read the passage and answer the questions below.

Passage: Ashton's Lesson

1   Ashton couldn't wait to get home from school to play the new video game system his parents got him for Christmas. It was all he could think about as he sat through his classes. In fact, when Mrs. Burghardt, his math teacher, asked him to answer a question in class, he was too busy daydreaming about fighting space aliens from the planet Dramilia to even know she was talking to him.

2   Embarrassed, he glanced at the faces of his classmates, their **ridicule** of his behavior clear by the way they whispered to each other and laughed quietly. Finally, he had to confess to Mrs. Burghardt that he didn't know the answer. She frowned before moving on to a girl next to him, Sammy Parker, who always knew the right answers.

3   "You were thinking about that game again, weren't you?" Ashton's friend Miguel said to him as they walked to their English class.

4   Ashton nodded.

5   Miguel shook his head. "Your parents are going to take it away if you're not more careful."

6   Ashton waved him off. "They wouldn't have got it for me if they didn't think I could handle it."

7   Miguel laughed. "Can you?"

8   Ashton shrugged. "Maybe I could pay more attention in math class."

9   That afternoon, Ashton spent the next several hours, from the moment he got home until he was too tired to keep going, playing his video game. He only took a break for a short dinner with his family.

10   His mom looked at him with **concern.** "I don't know if you should be playing those games so much, Sweetie," she said.

11   Ashton **conjured** his best smile. "I'm fine mom," he said. "The games are fun."

12   "You don't have any homework tonight?" she asked.

13   The memory of Mrs. Burghardt and her scratchy voice telling the class to do problems six through ten on page ninety-seven came to his mind like a mean witch **intent** on taking his fun away. "Not tonight," he said before running back to his room to finish the night playing.

14   The next day, when he failed to turn in his homework, Mrs. Burghardt kept him after class to talk to him.

15   "You've been **distracted** lately," she said softly. "What's keeping you from doing your best?"

16   Ashton just shrugged. He couldn't tell her that he spent all his time playing video games.

17   "I'm afraid I'm going to have to call your mom," his teacher said. "Not doing your homework is unacceptable for someone of your **capability,** Ashton."

18   Ashton felt panic rising in his body. If Mrs. Burghardt called his mom, he'd lose his video games for sure. He didn't fight, however. He knew his ship was sunk.

19   After being grounded for a month from his video games for lying about his homework, Ashton decided that playing a little time on his video games each day, instead of indulging all the time, was a **bright** idea.

1. Based on the sentence below, which of the following is the best definition of **ridicule?**
   *Embarrassed, he glanced at the faces of his classmates, their **ridicule** of his behavior clear by the way they whispered to each other and laughed quietly. (Paragraph 2)*
   - **A.** love
   - **B.** hate
   - **C.** teasing
   - **D.** enjoyment

2. Based on the sentences below, which of the following is the best definition of **concern?**
   *His mom looked at him with **concern**. "I don't know if you should be playing those games so much, Sweetie," she said. (Paragraph 10)*
   - **A.** confidence
   - **B.** love
   - **C.** fear
   - **D.** worry

3. Based on the text, which of the following is the best definition of **conjured?**
   - **A.** made appear
   - **B.** used magic
   - **C.** imagined
   - **D.** combined ingredients to form

4. Based on the text, which of the following is the best definition of **distracted?**
    A. focused
    B. unable to concentrate
    C. interested
    D. lazy

5. Based on the text, which of the following is the best definition of **capability?**
    A. potential
    B. disability
    C. interests
    D. weakness

6. The sentence below contains which type of figurative language?
   He knew his ship was sunk. (Paragraph 18)
    A. simile
    B. metaphor
    C. hyperbole
    D. personification

7. Based on the text, which of the following is the best definition of **bright?**
    A. shining
    B. happy
    C. clear
    D. good

8. Which of the following quotes from the text contains a simile?
    A. "It was all he could think about as he sat through his classes." (Paragraph 1)
    B. "Mrs. Burghardt and her scratchy voice telling the class to do problems six through ten on page ninety-seven came to his mind like a mean witch intent on taking his fun away." (Paragraph 13)
    C. "He knew his ship was sunk." (Paragraph 18)
    D. "After being grounded for a month from his video games for lying about his homework, Ashton decided that playing a little time on his video games each day, instead of indulging all the time, was a bright idea." (Paragraph 19)

ORGANIZATION

RL.5.5: Explain how a series of chapters, scenes, or stanzas fits together to provide the overall structure of a particular story, drama, or poem.

Directions: Read the passage and answer the questions that follow.

Passage 1: Adapted from *Riders to the Sea*
by John Millington Synge

CHARACTERS
MAURYA, an old woman
BARTLEY, her son
CATHLEEN, her daughter
NORA, a younger daughter
MEN AND WOMEN

1   [An island off the West of Ireland. Cottage kitchen, with nets, oilskins, spinning-wheel, some new boards standing by the wall, etc. CATHLEEN, a girl of about twenty, finishes kneading cake, and puts it down in the pot-oven by the fire; then wipes her hands, and begins to spin at the wheel. NORA, a young girl, puts her head in at the door.]

2   NORA: (in a low voice) Where is she?

3   CATHLEEN: She's lying down, and maybe sleeping, if she's able.

4   [NORA comes in softly, and takes a bundle from under her shawl.]

5   CATHLEEN: (spinning the wheel rapidly): Is the sea bad by the white rocks, Nora?

6   NORA: Kind of bad. There's a great roaring in the west, and it's worse it'll be getting when the tide's turned to the wind. [She goes over to the table with the bundle.] Shall I open it now?

7   CATHLEEN: Maybe Maura will wake up on us, and come in before we'd done. [Coming to the table] It's a long time we'll be, and the two of us looking.

8   NORA: (goes to the inner door and listens) She's moving about on the bed. She'll be coming in a minute.

9   CATHLEEN: Give me the ladder, and I'll put the surprise in the turf-loft, that way she won't know about it at all, and maybe when the tide turns she'll be going down to see the waves.

10   [They put the ladder against the gable of the chimney; CATHLEEN goes up a few steps and hides the bundle in the turf-loft. MAURYA comes from the inner room.]

READING: LITERATURE

11   MAURYA: (looking up at CATHLEEN and speaking fussily) Do you have enough food for this day and evening?

12   CATHLEEN: There's a cake baking at the fire for a short time, and Bartley will want it when the tide turns if he goes to Connemara.

13   [NORA picks up the other food and puts it around the pot-oven.]

14   MAURYA: (sitting down on a stool at the fire) He won't go this day with the wind rising from the south and west. He won't go this day, for the young priest will stop him surely.

15   NORA: He'll not stop him, mother, and I heard Eamon Simon and Stephen Pheety and Colum Shawn saying he would go.

16   MAURYA: Where is he, anyway?

17   NORA: He went down to see of there would be another boat sailing in the week, and I'm thinking it won't be long till he's here now, for the tide's turning at the green head.

18   CATHLEEN: I hear someone passing the big stones.

19   NORA: (looking out) He's coming now, and he in a hurry.

20   BARTLEY: (comes in and looks round the room; speaking sadly and quietly) Where is the bit of new rope, Cathleen, was bought in Connemara?

21   CATHLEEN: (coming down) Give it to him, Nora; it's on a nail by the white boards. I hung it up this morning, for the pig with the black feet was eating it.

22   NORA: (giving him a rope) Is that it, Bartley?

23   MAURYA: You'd do right to leave that rope, Bartley, hanging by the boards. (BARTLEY takes the rope.)

24   BARTLEY: (beginning to work with the rope) I've no halter to ride down on the mare, and I must go now quickly. This is the one boat going for two weeks or beyond it, and the fair will be a good fair for horses, I heard them saying below.

1. This question has two parts. First, answer Part A. Then, answer Part B.

Part A
What is the purpose of Paragraph 1?
> **A.** to describe the setting
> **B.** to tell what has happened in the past
> **C.** to tell how Maurya is different from the other characters
> **D.** to preview what is about to happen

Part B

Which other paragraph provides more information to Paragraph 1?

    A. Paragraph 3

    B. Paragraph 15

    C. Paragraph 19

    D. Paragraph 9

2. A character in the play is baking a cake and hiding a bundle in the turf-loft. What do these actions indicate the character is doing?

    A.   celebrating a birthday

    B.   mourning a loss

    C.   preparing to move

    D.   welcoming new neighbors

3. How does Cathleen's question asking whether the sea is bad (Paragraph 5) connect to a later event in the passage?

    A. She is asking about the sea because her friend is currently on a boat.

    B. She is asking about the sea because her mother wants her to go down to the seaside and look for seashells.

    C. She is asking about the sea because she knows her brother wants to go traveling on a boat.

    D. She is asking about the sea because she may need to board up the windows if bad weather is coming.

4. How does the list of characters (before Paragraph 1) help readers to understand the play?

    A. Readers can understand how characters get along.

    B. Readers can understand who the characters are and how they are related in the family.

    C. Readers can become aware of who is in charge.

    D. None of the above

5. What is the purpose of the words inside parentheses? (Refer to Paragraphs 2 and 5).

    A. The words inside parentheses show actions being completed by the character.

    B. The words indicate that the character is entering the stage.

    C. The words indicate that the character is exiting the stage.

    D. None of the above

A Jelly-Fish
by Marianne Moore

Visible, invisible,
A fluctuating charm,
An amber-colored amethyst
Inhabits it; your arm
Approaches, and
It opens and
It closes;
You have meant
To catch it,
And it shrivels;
You abandon
Your intent—
It opens, and it
Closes and you
Reach for it—
The blue
Surrounding it
Grows cloudy, and
It floats away
From you.

6. Which statement accurately describes the jellyfish's story throughout the poem?
    A. The jellyfish gets trapped in a net.
    B. The jellyfish is there, and then it isn't.
    C. The jellyfish opens and closes, attacks, and then floats away.
    D. The jellyfish changes colors.

7. The first line says that the jellyfish is "visible, invisible". Which line in the poem best supports that the jellyfish can no longer be viewed?
    A. "Grows cloudy, and"
    B. "It opens, and it"
    C. "Reach for it—"
    D. "An amber-colored amethyst"

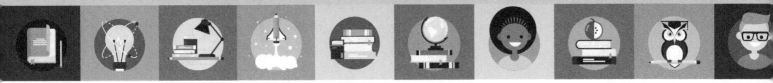

8. Use at two details from the poem to provide some facts you learned about the jellyfish.

_____

_____

_____

_____

_____

_____

_____

_____

DESCRIBE HOW POINT OF VIEW INFLUENCES EVENTS

RL.5.6 Describe how a narrator's or speaker's point of view influences how events are described.

Directions: Read the passages and answer the questions below.

Passage 1: Emily's Night

1   The crash of thunder stirred Emily out of a peaceful sleep. She jumped out of bed and ran to her parent's room. They were still sound asleep.

2   "Mommy," she whispered, nudging her mom.

3   Her mom groaned. "What's wrong, Em?"

4   "Thunder," Emily whispered, her voice a little shaky.

5   Her mom turned over. "It's just a storm," she said. "It'll pass." She patted Emily's back. "Just go back to sleep. Everything is fine."

6   Emily dragged her feet as she walked away from her parent's bed. The sound of rain pounding on the window and another sharp crack of thunder caused her to stop and turn around.

7   "Can I sleep with you?" she said, already climbing onto the bed and crawling into the space between her mom and dad.

8   Her mom pulled back the covers. "Sure," she whispered.

9   The thunder and rain continued, but Emily the slept the rest of the night through it.

1. Who is the narrator of the story in Passage 1?
  - **A.** An outside observer
  - **B.** Emily
  - **C.** Emily's mom
  - **D.** Emily's dad

2. This question has two parts. First, answer Part A. Then, answer Part B.

Part A
How does Emily feel about the rain?
  - **A.** She is excited about it.
  - **B.** She finds it relaxing.
  - **C.** She is afraid of it.
  - **D.** She isn't affected by it.

Part B

Which of the following details from the text best supports your answer in Part A?

    A. "They were sound asleep." (Paragraph 1)

    B. "'Mommy,' she whispered, nudging her mom." (Paragraph 2)

    C. "'Thunder,' Emily whispered, her voice a little shaky." (Paragraph 4)

    D. "The thunder and rain continued, but Emily the slept the rest of the night through it." (Paragraph 9)

3. How would the story be different if it were told from the perspective of Emily's mom?

_____

_____

_____

_____

_____

4. How old do you believe Emily is in the story? Use evidence from the text to support your response.

_____

_____

_____

_____

_____

Passage 2: Muddy Puddles

1   The rain had just started when I curled up in a chair next to my bedroom window. The sun was still out, but only just barely. Rain drops tapped lightly on my window, a sound that made my head start to nod, but I struggled to stay awake.

2   As I read my book, the rain continued. I heard a long low rumble of thunder and it reminded me about time my friends and I ran outside in our bare feet in the rain and started jumping around in the muddy puddles.

3   "Get back inside," my mother snapped as soon as she noticed.

4   My friends and I laughed as we ran back inside. We were freezing cold for the next thirty minutes, but that didn't stop us from doing it again the next time it rained.

5   I closed my book and put it aside. I noticed a puddle forming in the front yard and decided it had been too long since I'd run out into the rain to play.

5. Who is the narrator of the story in Passage 2?
> **A.** an outside observer
> **B.** the main character who is telling her own story
> **C.** the main character's mom
> **D.** the main character's friends

6. This question has two parts. First, answer Part A. Then, answer Part B.

Part A
How does the narrator feel about the rain?
> **A.** She is afraid of it.
> **B.** She loves it.
> **C.** She doesn't mind it.
> **D.** She doesn't notice it.

Part B
Which of the following details from the text best supports your answer in Part A?
> **A.** "The rain had just started when I curled up in a chair next to my bedroom window." (Paragraph 1)
> **B.** "Rain drops tapped lightly on my window, a sound that made my head start to nod, but I struggled to stay awake." (Paragraph 1)
> **C.** "'Get back inside,' my mother snapped as soon as she noticed." (Paragraph 3)
> **D.** "I noticed a puddle forming in the front yard and decided it had been too long since I'd run out into the rain to play." (Paragraph 5)

7. How do the differing perspectives in Passage 1 and Passage 2 influence how a similar event is described?

_____

_____

_____

_____

_____

8. How might the story in Passage 2 be different if it were told from the perspective of Emily from Passage 1?

_____

_____

_____

_____

_____

ANALYZE HOW IMAGES CONTRIBUTE TO TEXT

RL.5.7 Analyze how visual and multimedia elements contribute to the meaning, tone, or beauty of a text (e.g., graphic novel, multimedia presentation of fiction, folktale, myth, poem).

Directions: Read the passage and answer the questions below.

Passage 1: The Town Mouse and the Country Mouse

1   A Town Mouse once visited a relative who lived in the country. For lunch the Country Mouse served wheat stalks, roots, and acorns, with a dash of cold water for drink. The Town Mouse ate very sparingly, nibbling a little of this and a little of that, and by her manner making it very plain that she ate the simple food only to be polite.

2   After the meal the friends had a long talk, or rather the Town Mouse talked about her life in the city while the Country Mouse listened. They then went to bed in a cozy nest in the hedgerow and slept in quiet and comfort until morning. In her sleep the Country Mouse dreamed she was a Town Mouse with all the luxuries and delights of city life that her friend had described for her. So the next day when the Town Mouse asked the Country Mouse to go home with her to the city, she gladly said yes.

3   When they reached the mansion in which the Town Mouse lived, they found on the table in the dining room the leavings of a very fine banquet. There were sweetmeats and jellies, pastries, delicious cheeses, indeed, the most tempting foods that a Mouse can imagine. But just as the Country Mouse was about to nibble a dainty bit of pastry, she heard a Cat mew loudly and scratch at the door. In great fear the Mice scurried to a hiding place, where they lay quite still for a long time, hardly daring to breathe. When at last they ventured back to the feast, the door opened suddenly and in came the servants to clear the table, followed by the House Dog.

4   The Country Mouse stopped in the Town Mouse's den only long enough to pick up her carpet bag and umbrella.

5   "You may have luxuries and dainties that I have not," she said as she hurried away, "but I prefer my plain food and simple life in the country with the peace and security that go with it."

Figure 1

1. Which of the following words best describes the tone of paragraphs 1 and 2 in Passage 1?

   A. suspenseful

   B. lighthearted

   C. humorous

   D. gloomy

2. How does the tone in Passage 1 shift in the middle of paragraph 3?

   A. from optimistic to frightened

   B. from tense to relaxed

   C. from fearful to relieved

   D. from humorous to serious

3. How is the tone of Passage 1 enhanced by the image in Figure 1?

   A. It contrasts with what actually happens in the passage.

   B. It increases the intensity in paragraph 3.

   C. It anticipates the tragic way the story ends.

   D. It suggests a playfulness in the passage.

4. Describe the differences between living in the town and the country. Use details from the text to support your answer.

   _____

   _____

   _____

   _____

   _____

Passage 2: The Hare and the Tortoise

1   A Hare was making fun of the Tortoise one day for being so slow.

2   "Do you ever get anywhere?" he asked with a mocking laugh.

3   "Yes," replied the Tortoise, "and I get there sooner than you think. I'll run you a race and prove it."

4   The Hare was much amused at the idea of running a race with the Tortoise, but for the fun of the thing he agreed. So the Fox, who had consented to act as judge, marked the distance and started the runners off.

5   The Hare was soon far out of sight, and to make the Tortoise feel very deeply how ridiculous it was for him to try a race with a Hare, he lay down beside the course to take a nap until the Tortoise should catch up.

6   The Tortoise meanwhile kept going slowly but steadily, and, after a time, passed the place where the Hare was sleeping. But the Hare slept on very peacefully; and when at last he did wake up, the Tortoise was near the goal. The Hare now ran his swiftest, but he could not overtake the Tortoise in time.

Figure 2

Figure 3

5. Which of the following words best describes the overall tone and message of Passage 2?
    A. humored
    B. cautionary
    C. dreadful
    D. peaceful

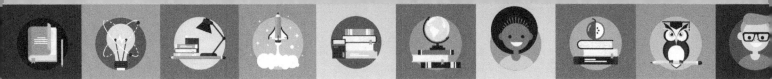

6. Look at the image in Figure 2. Describe where you believe it belongs in Passage 2.

_____

_____

_____

_____

_____

7. How does the image in Figure 2 *enhance* the story in Passage 2?
   A. It shows the Hare sleeping.
   B. It demonstrates the speed at which the Tortoise was moving.
   C. It reveals the Tortoise's amusement at passing the sleeping Hare.
   D. It shows the Hare's exhaustion from trying to defeat the Tortoise.

8. Which of the following is NOT a theme communicated by Passage 2 and the images in Figure 2 and 3?
   A. Never underestimate your opponent.
   B. Everyone's abilities are equal.
   C. Being better at something isn't a reason to look down on someone.
   D. Give your best even when you have an advantage.

COMPARE & CONTRAST STORIES IN SAME GENRE

RL.5.9 Compare and contrast stories in the same genre (e.g., mysteries and adventure stories) on their approaches to similar themes and topics.

Directions: Read the passages and answer the questions below.

Passage 1: Jared's Chance

1   Jared glanced at the scoreboard one last time before stepping up to the plate. It was the bottom of the ninth inning, and his team, the Bluejays, were one point behind. With the last two batters getting struck out, tying the game was up to him.

2   Jared positioned himself to swing just before the pitcher threw his first pitch, a low fastball. He swung hard, expecting to feel the impact of his bat with the ball.

3   "Strike one!" the umpire called out.

4   Disappointed, Jared looked to the stands where his father was sitting. His father's face looked stern, and Jared could imagine what his dad would say if Jared struck out.

5   "I knew you'd choke," he'd probably say. "Remember the last time your team depended on you?"

6   Jared got ready for the next pitch. He had to hit the ball. He had to prove he was a winner.

7   The pitch came, and he swung.

8   "Strike two!" the umpire yelled.

9   Jared groaned as he got back into position. He looked over at his father again, but this time his father wasn't even looking.

10   The third pitch came, and Jared swung. Jared wasn't expecting the feel of the bat connecting with the ball, so when he looked into the stands and saw the look of hope in his father's eyes and then the sight of the ball soaring toward the fence in right field, he knew his moment had come.

11   Jared raced toward first base, filled with joy. He'd done it.

12   His excitement was interrupted by the umpire calling, "Out!"

13   Jared stopped in disbelief. That was when he noticed the right fielder holding the ball in his hand.

14   Jared looked back at the stands to see his father walking away toward the car. The game was over.

15   Jared's team had lost. At that moment, Jared not only wanted the game to be over, but all of baseball season.

Passage 2: Playing the Moment

1   Trey ran out onto the baseball field with his team, determined to play the best game of his life. He'd spent the entire season pitching after moving from second base the previous season, and he'd had a blast the entire time.

2   As he stepped onto the mound to take the first pitch, he thought about the advice his father had given him when they were practicing the night before.

3   "Winning is a fun part of the game, son," he said, "but it's only part of it." He'd said it after Trey was getting frustrated that he couldn't get his curve ball to land in the strike zone. "Being named the winner is only a moment at the end of a game," his father continued. "Don't lose sight of enjoying all the moments you're actually playing the game."

4   Trey smiled at the memory and gave his dad a look in the stands. He wound up and threw his first pitch, the curve ball, and could barely hold in his excitement when the batter swung and missed.

5   Win or lose, Trey was going to play the best game of his life.

1. Which of the following is NOT something the two passages have in common?
    A. the game of baseball
    B. the influence of fathers
    C. competing in a game of baseball
    D. a team winning a game of baseball

2. This question has two parts. First, answer Part A. Then, answer Part B.

Part A
Which of the following best describes how Jared feels about playing baseball in Passage 1?
    A. It's a relaxing pastime.
    B. He cares more about playing than winning.
    C. Winning is more important than anything.
    D. He wishes he could quit playing.

Part B

Which of the following details best supports your answer in Part B?

- **A.** "With the last two batters getting struck out, tying the game was up to him." (Paragraph 1)
- **B.** "Jared got ready for the next pitch. He had to hit the ball. He had to prove he was a winner." (Paragraph 6)
- **C.** "Jared wasn't expecting the feel of the bat connecting with the ball, so when he looked into the stands and saw the look of hope in his father's eyes and then the sight of the ball soaring toward the fence in right field, he knew his moment had come." (Paragraph 10)
- **D.** "Jared looked back at the stands to see his father walking away toward the car. The game was over." (Paragraph 14)

3. This question has two parts. First, answer Part A. Then, answer Part B.

Part A

Which of the following best describes how Trey feels about playing baseball in Passage 2?

- A. He's determined to win more than anything.
- B. He enjoys playing, whether he wins or loses.
- C. He only plays because his dad makes him.
- D. He enjoys playing, but it's not his favorite thing to do.

Part B

Which of the following details BEST supports your answer in Part B?

- **A.** "Trey ran out onto the baseball field with his team, determined to play the best game of his life." (Paragraph 1)
- **B.** "As he stepped onto the mound to take the first pitch, he thought about the advice his father had given him when they were practicing the night before." (Paragraph 2)
- **C.** "He wound up and threw his first pitch, the curve ball, and could barely hold in his excitement when the batter swung and missed." (Paragraph 4)
- **D.** "Win or lose, Trey was going to play the best game of his life."

4. Which of the following best describes the relationships each of the boys in both passages have with their fathers?

- **A.** Jared knows his father supports him while Trey struggles to make his father happy.
- **B.** Jared fears disappointing his father while Trey knows his father loves him even if he loses.
- **C.** Both boys are driven to please their fathers, but only find disappointment in the end.
- **D.** Both boys are inspired by supportive fathers to do their best.

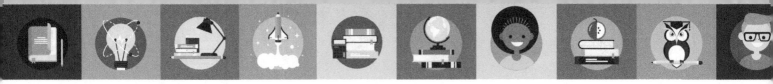

5. What most influences how each character, Jared and Trey, feels about playing baseball? Use details from the passage to support your answer.

_____

_____

_____

_____

_____

6. Which of the following reasons do you think best describes why Passage 2 ends without revealing to the reader how the game ended?

   A. The author wanted to focus on the beginning of the game rather than the end.

   B. The author felt that not revealing the outcome of the game fit the story's theme that winning or losing wasn't as important enjoying the game itself.

   C. The author thought that the reader would be disappointed if Trey lost the game.

   D. The author thought that Trey would lose focus on enjoying the game if he won the game.

7. How might have Jared's approach to baseball been different if he had Trey's father instead of his own?

_____

_____

_____

_____

_____

8. Together, which of the following best communicates a theme communicated by the two stories?

   A. It doesn't matter if you win or lose; it only matters how you play the game.

   B. People aren't influenced by the people around them; they do what makes them happy.

   C. Baseball is a great way to make people respect you.

   D. Fathers can have a powerful influence in the lives of their sons.

READING: INFORMATION

QUOTE ACCURATELY AND DRAW INFERENCES FROM A TEXT

RI.5.1 Quote accurately from a text when explaining what the text says explicitly and when drawing inferences from the text.

Directions: Read the passage and answer the questions below.

Passage 1: Mansa Musa

1   Mansa Musa was the king of the Mali Empire in West Africa in the 14th century, and historians believe he was the wealthiest person in the history of the world. Mansa Musa made his fortune from the lucrative natural resources in his land, such as ivory, salt, and gold.

2   Mansa Musa's real name was Musa Keita I. When he ascended to the throne in 1312, he was given the name Mansa, meaning king. As king, Mansa Musa was known for more than just his wealth. He expanded the borders of the Mali Empire, advanced education, and constructed many important buildings.

3   Mansa Musa oversaw the construction of several schools, including the University of Timbuktu, sometimes called Sankore University. Many scholars believe that the University of Timbuktu was the world's first university. Mansa Musa's reign brought years of peace and prosperity to West Africa.

4   Despite his many achievements, Mansa Musa is perhaps best known for his astonishing wealth. Today, Mansa Musa's fortune would be worth an estimated $400 billion. Even this number may not be accurate—Time reporter Jacob Davidson states that Musa was "richer than anyone could describe...There's really no way to put an accurate number on his wealth."

5   Mansa Musa traveled around the world, usually with a crowd of hundreds of thousands of people, all dressed in the finest silks. Horses and camels carrying countless bars of gold were also part of his processions.

6   When Mansa Musa visited the Egyptian city of Cairo, he spent so much money and donated so much to the poor that he caused mass inflation. It took the city of Cairo years to completely recover from his visit.

7   However, Mansa Musa did his best to help. On his way back through Cairo, Musa tried to rectify the gold market by borrowing all the gold he could from Cairo's money-lenders, at high interest. This is the only time in recorded history that one man directly controlled the price of gold in the Mediterranean.

8   The world took notice of Mansa Musa and the Mali Empire as a result of these journeys. Even far-off European kings heard tales of the wealthy king and his luxurious travels. On

many maps from this time period, drawings of Mansa Musa, usually with gold coins, are placed near Mali's location.

9   Mansa Musa's trips weren't just for entertainment: the king also recruited architects, scholars, and other important people to return to Mali with him. As a result, his reign brought culture, architecture, trade, wealth, and education to the Mali Empire.

10   The date of Musa's death is debated by scholars. However, most believe that he died around 1337, after ruling for 25 years. His descendants were not able to maintain his fortune, but many libraries and buildings still stand as a testament to the golden age of Mansa Musa's reign.

1. This question has two parts. First, answer Part A. Then, answer Part B.

Part A
What happened to Mansa Musa's fortune after his death?

    A. It was donated to build libraries and important buildings.

    B. It was inherited by his descendants, who increased it.

    C. Mansa Musa's fortune was stolen from the Mali Empire.

    D. Mansa Musa's descendants lost most of his fortune.

Part B
Which quote from the text best supports your answer in Part A?

    A. "Today, Mansa Musa's fortune would be worth an estimated $400 billion." (Paragraph 4)

    B. "His descendants were not able to maintain his fortune, but many libraries and buildings still stand as a testament to the golden age of Mansa Musa's reign." (Paragraph 9)

    C. "On many maps from this time period, drawings of Mansa Musa, usually with gold coins, are placed near Mali's location." (Paragraph 8)

    D. "Mansa Musa made his fortune from the lucrative natural resources in his land, such as ivory, salt, and gold." (Paragraph 1)

2. During his reign, Mansa Musa made history by being the first person to achieve several accomplishments. List two quotes from the text that support this statement.

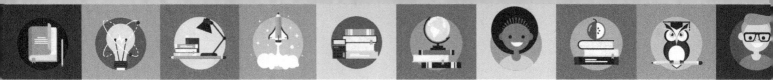

3. Other than being extremely wealthy, what were some of Mansa Musa's contributions to the Mali Empire? Quote evidence from the text to support your answer.

_____

_____

_____

_____

_____

4. This question has two parts. First, answer Part A. Then, answer Part B.

Part A
How did Mansa Musa's journeys benefit the Mali Empire?

   A. They brought recognition and important people to the empire.

   B. They impressed everyone around the world.

   C. They gave Mansa Musa the opportunity to learn from scholars and architects.

   D. They brought even more money to the wealthy empire.

Part B
Which of the following quotes from the text BEST supports your answer in Part A?

   A. "When Mansa Musa visited the Egyptian city of Cairo, he spent so much money and donated so much to the poor that he caused mass inflation." (Paragraph 6)

   B. "Mansa Musa's trips weren't just for entertainment: the king also recruited architects, scholars, and other important people to return to Mali with him." (Paragraph 9)

   C. "Mansa Musa traveled around the world, usually with a crowd of hundreds of thousands of people, all dressed in the finest silks. Horses and camels carrying countless bars of gold were also part of his processions." (Paragraph 5)

   D. "On many maps from this time period, drawings of Mansa Musa, usually with gold coins, are placed near Mali's location." (Paragraph 8)

Directions: Read the passage and answer the questions below.

Passage 2: Alexander the Great

1   Although Alexander the Great only lived to the age of 32, he is considered one of history's most powerful leaders and most dominant military minds. Even other legendary rulers like Julius Caesar, Napoleon, and Charlemagne attempted to follow Alexander the Great's example.

2   At the young age of twelve, Alexander tamed a dangerous stallion that no one else could ride, not even the greatest men in the kingdom. Witnessing this achievement, his father cried tears of joy. He knew that his kingdom would continue to prosper after his death. Alexander rode the stallion, named Bucephalus, in his major battles later in life.

3   Alexander the Great rose to the throne of the Ancient Greek kingdom of Macedon at age 20. Immediately, he ordered the executions of all of his enemies. After the death of Alexander's father, nations that had been conquered by Macedon attempted to rebel. To show that he would not be a weak king, Alexander swiftly put down these rebellions and executed their leaders.

4   The famous philosopher Aristotle had been Alexander's tutor, so he learned to be a brilliant military strategist. He was also known for his superior speed in battle. By the age of only 26, Alexander had conquered the Persian Empire. As a result of his military campaigns, Greek culture spread as far as Asia.

5   Although he was very successful, Alexander was not a popular or beloved king. He had a terrible temper, drank too much wine, and was ruthless to anyone who dared oppose him— even his friends. Many of Alexander's subjects thought he was too ambitious and conquered other nations merely for the sake of conquering, with no real purpose.

6   After suffering a high fever for ten days, Alexander died at the age of 32. The exact cause of the fever is unknown, but theories include malaria, typhoid fever, or even poison. By the time he died, Alexander the Great had conquered territory in Egypt, India, Turkey, Iran, Syria, and Mesopotamia. In fact, he had conquered most of the world that was known to the Ancient Greeks during that time period. He also died undefeated in battle, marking him as a legendary military strategist.

5. Why did Alexander the Great's father cry tears of joy after Alexander rode Bucephalus?
   Use quotes from the text to support your answer.

_____

_____

_____

_____

_____

6. This question has two parts. First, answer Part A. Then, answer Part B.

Part A

Why did other leaders like Charlemagne and Julius Caesar try to follow Alexander the
Great's example?

    A. He was admired and respected by his subjects.

    B. He was intelligent and generous.

    C. He was a brilliant military leader.

    D. He was extremely wealthy.

Part B

Which quotation from the text best supports your answer in Part A?

    A. "At the young age of twelve, Alexander tamed a dangerous stallion that no one
        else could ride, not even the greatest men in the kingdom." (Paragraph 2)

    B. "Many of Alexander's subjects thought he was too ambitious and conquered
        other nations merely for the sake of conquering, with no real purpose."
        (Paragraph 5)

    C. "By the time he died, Alexander the Great had conquered territory in Egypt,
        India, Turkey, Iran, Syria, and Mesopotamia. In fact, he had conquered most
        of the world that was known to the Ancient Greeks during that time period."
        (Paragraph 6)

    D. "Alexander the Great rose to the throne of the Ancient Greek kingdom of
        Macedon at age 20. Immediately, he ordered the executions of all of his
        enemies." (Paragraph 3)

7. One theory about Alexander the Great's early death is that he was poisoned. Select two
quotes from the text that show someone may have wanted to poison Alexander.

_____

_____

_____

_____

8. Alexander achieved a great deal at a young age. Select two quotes from the text that
support this statement.

_____

_____

_____

_____

_____

DETERMINE MAIN IDEA AND SUMMARIZE TEXT

RI.5.2 Determine two or more main ideas of a text and explain how they are supported by key details; summarize the text.

1   You probably know that people have five senses. But did you know that some people experience blended senses, known as synesthesia? People who have synesthesia, called synesthetes, may be able to taste letters of the alphabet or visualize songs and noises as certain colors.

2   Synesthesia is both involuntary and consistent. This means synesthetes can't control their blended perception. They also experience sensations consistently. For instance, if a certain song sounds purple to someone, it will still sound purple the next time they hear it, and every time after that. However, sensations can sometimes change over a period of several years.

3   Sometimes, a synesthete will link two particular senses, like seeing colors every time they hear music, or tasting something when they see letters. In some rare cases, synesthetes can experience all five senses at once. A noise might come with a color, smell, taste, a feeling of hot or cold, etc.

4   Living with synesthesia can sometimes be challenging, confusing, and overwhelming. Trying to solve math problems, for example, can be distracting when you perceive the numbers as different colors. This forces synesthetes to process a variety of sensations at once. On the other hand, many synesthetes view synesthesia as a gift that makes life brighter and more interesting.

5   According to research, about four in every 100 people experience synesthesia. These people, including musicians Billy Joel and Pharrell Williams, may see sounds or smell colors. Currently, scientists aren't sure how this happens. Depending on which senses are being blended, the brain reacts in a few different ways. As brain imaging technology and research continue to advance, scientists may soon learn more.

1. Which of the following is the main idea of Passage 1?
    A. While some synesthetes think synesthesia is challenging, others enjoy it.
    B. About four in every 100 people experience synesthesia.
    C. Synesthesia causes people to involuntarily, consistently experience blended senses.
    D. Scientists aren't sure what causes synesthesia yet.

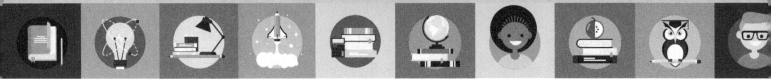

2. Which two sentences could best be included in a summary of Passage 1?

☐ **1** Living with synesthesia can sometimes be challenging, confusing, and overwhelming.

☐ **2** Synesthesia is both involuntary and consistent.

☐ **3** However, sensations can sometimes change over a period of several years.

☐ **4** Trying to solve math problems, for example, can be distracting when you perceive the numbers as different colors.

☐ **5** People who have synesthesia, called synesthetes, may be able to taste letters of the alphabet or visualize songs and noises as certain colors.

☐ **6** For instance, if a certain song sounds purple to someone, it will still sound purple the next time they hear it, and every time after that.

3. One main idea in the text is that we still need additional research on synesthesia. List two details from the text that support this idea.

_____

_____

_____

_____

_____

4. People living with synesthesia have mixed feelings about the condition. Select the answer choice that best supports this statement.

A. "Depending on which senses are being blended, the brain reacts in a few different ways." (Paragraph 5)

B. "On the other hand, many synesthetes view synesthesia as a gift that makes life brighter and more interesting." (Paragraph 4)

C. "Trying to solve math problems, for example, can be distracting when you perceive the numbers as different colors." (Paragraph 4)

D. "Sometimes, a synesthete will link two particular senses, like seeing colors every time they hear music, or tasting something when they see letters." (Paragraph 3)

Directions: Read the passage and answer the questions below.

Passage 2: The Power of Words: The American Revolution

1   The American Revolution stemmed from American colonists feeling that they had no freedom under British rule. At the same time, some colonists weren't sure if they supported the fight for independence. In the end, the power of words convinced many people that a revolution was necessary.

2   Patriots like Samuel Adams, Thomas Jefferson, and Patrick Henry made powerful statements that changed the minds of many colonists. These quotable words included, "No taxation without representation!" and, "Give me liberty or give me death!" Later, more powerful words—those in the Declaration of Independence and Articles of Confederation—created the United States.

3   The Declaration of Independence, signed in 1776, was largely a list of complaints against the English king. Throughout the 1770s, the relationship between England and the American colonies had been growing worse. The colonies called for a series of meetings, which culminated in the signing of the Declaration of Independence on July 4, 1776.

4   The document stated that governments exist to ensure the freedom and liberty of their people. Governments also draw their power from the people, according to the Declaration. Since the American colonists felt the British government had trampled on their rights, they had the right to declare their independence from England.

5   Unsurprisingly, the British didn't agree. They sent troops in an effort to stop the colonists' rebellion. Although the war lasted until 1783, the American colonists formed their new government before it ended. A document called the Articles of Confederation united the 13 colonies and formed the first government of the new sovereign nation. The document was written the same year as the Declaration of Independence, but it was approved by the states in 1781. This was the United States' first Constitution.

6   At first, the new government wasn't successful. States disagreed over topics like taxes and boundary lines. The economy was weak, and many people owed large amounts of money. Farmers especially struggled. Their crops had been destroyed during the revolution, they owed large sums of money, and they were being asked to pay high taxes.

7   In 1786, angry farmers in Massachusetts revolted against the government in what became known as Shays' Rebellion. The Massachusetts militia eventually ended the rebellion, but it was a sign of the new government's inability to maintain order.

8   In response, Alexander Hamilton began organizing a meeting in Philadelphia in 1787. This convention ultimately threw out the Articles of Confederation and crafted the

Constitution that we know today. Hamilton knew that a stronger government was needed, and the Constitution achieved this goal.

9   The Constitution created a perfect balance between freedom and order in the fledgling United States, and the chaos died down. In the end, our nation's independence and government began with the power of words.

5. What is the main idea of Passage 2? Use at least two details from the text to support your response.

_____

_____

_____

_____

_____

6. This question has two parts. First, answer Part A. Then, answer Part B.

Part A
Why were the Articles of Confederation rewritten?
> **A.** They were unfair.
> **B.** The English government didn't approve of them.
> **C.** They created a weak government, resulting in chaos.
> **D.** Because the economy was extremely poor.

Part B
Which of the following details from the text BEST supports your answer in Part A?
> **A.** "Unsurprisingly, the British didn't agree. They sent troops in an effort to stop the colonists' rebellion." (Paragraph 5)
> **B.** "At first, the new government wasn't successful. States disagreed over topics like taxes and boundary lines. The economy was weak, and many people owed large amounts of money." (Paragraph 6)
> **C.** "This convention ultimately threw out the Articles of Confederation and crafted the Constitution that we know today. Hamilton knew that a stronger government was needed, and the Constitution achieved this goal." (Paragraph 8)
> **D.** "Their crops had been destroyed during the revolution, they owed large sums of money, and they were being asked to pay high taxes." (Paragraph 6)

7. Which of the following is the best summary of Passage 2?

    A. The United States government struggled initially, but its problems were eventually resolved.

    B. The power of words played a major role in the American Revolution and the establishment of a United States government.

    C. Shays' Rebellion caused important changes to America's fledgling government.

    D. American colonists sought independence because they felt the British government wasn't giving them freedom.

8. This question has two parts. First, answer Part A. Then, answer Part B.

Part A

How was the Constitution different from the Articles of Confederation?

    A. It established stronger laws to maintain order.

    B. It united the thirteen colonies for the first time.

    C. It outlawed rebellions and revolutions in response to Shays' Rebellion.

    D. It gave the United States its freedom.

Part B

Which of the following details from the text best supports your answer in Part A?

    A. "In 1786, angry farmers in Massachusetts revolted against the government in what became known as Shays' Rebellion." (Paragraph 7)

    B. "A document called the Articles of Confederation united the 13 colonies and formed the first government of the new sovereign nation." (Paragraph 5)

    C. "At first, the new government wasn't successful. States disagreed over topics like taxes and boundary lines. The economy was weak, and many people owed large amounts of money." (Paragraph 6)

    D. "The Constitution created a perfect balance between freedom and order in the fledgling United States, and the chaos died down." (Paragraph 9)

EXPLAIN RELATIONSHIPS BETWEEN INDIVIDUALS, EVENTS, AND IDEAS IN TEXTS

RI.5.3 Explain the relationships or interactions between two or more individuals, events, ideas, or concepts in a historical, scientific, or technical text based on specific information in the text.

Directions: Read the passage and answer the questions below.

Passage 1: The United States' First Transcontinental Railroad

1   In the 1800s, American settlers began traveling west to establish homes in new territory. After gold was discovered in California, even more settlers journeyed westward, hoping to profit. Settlers traveled cross-country in covered wagons, and the trip was long, challenging, and dangerous.

2   In 1860, a young engineer named Theodore Judah decided to find a better way to travel across the country. He wanted to build a railroad across the Donner Pass, a path crossing the Sierra Nevada Mountains in California. Judah hoped that constructing this railroad would make it easier for settlers to travel across the country and for people to visit family and friends.

3   To complete his railroad, Judah started the Central Pacific Railroad Company. He traveled to Washington, D.C., where he convinced President Abraham Lincoln and other members of the government to support his project. Later, the government passed the Pacific Railroad Act.

4   The Pacific Railroad Act was designed to speed up the railroad project. It stated that Judah's Central Pacific Railroad Company would start building in Sacramento, California and continue east. Another company, the Union Pacific Railroad, would start from Omaha, Nebraska. For every mile of track each company built, the government would give them land and money. The two railroad companies began competing with one another to build as much of the track as possible, so that they could get more land and money.

5   Initially, the Union Pacific couldn't make much progress because of the Civil War. The war ended in 1865, and by 1866 the company finally started moving. They were attacked by Native Americans repeatedly, but they still moved quickly through the plains building their tracks.

6   On the other hand, the Central Pacific Company moved much slower. This was because they had to build through the mountains. In 1865, Central Pacific began hiring Chinese workers to do dangerous work in the mountains. Workers had to blast tunnels through the

granite, and sometimes they made only a two- or three-inch dent in the mountain by the end of the day.

7   Later, workers started using nitroglycerin to speed up the process, but this was far more dangerous. Some workers died from nitroglycerin explosions. Snow, wind, and bad weather often slowed the work down too.

8   By 1867, thousands of Chinese workers were employed by Central Pacific. The Union Pacific was moving faster than the Central Pacific, but Central Pacific finally broke through the mountains in June of 1867, putting the most difficult part behind them.

9   As the companies rushed to complete the railroad, workers built weak tracks that had to be rebuilt later. At the beginning of 1869, the companies were very close to one another. President Ulysses Grant had them decide where the railroads would meet, and they decided on Promontory Summit in Utah.

10   On May 10, 1869 the two tracks met, and the first transcontinental railroad in the United States was complete. The railroad made an almost immediate impact on life in the United States. People could travel much faster for less money, and goods could be bought and sold cross-country too. As Americans began to travel more freely, ideas were exchanged and business was conducted across the country. Even more settlers traveled westward.

11   On the other hand, the construction of the railroad did lead to the destruction of many natural resources. The railroad also severely damaged the Native American lifestyle as it pushed through tribal lands.

1. Why did the government pass the Pacific Railroad Act?
   A. To support Theodore Judah in his plan to construct a transcontinental railroad.
   B. To make the construction of the transcontinental railroad faster.
   C. To give the Union Pacific Railroad company the right to construct the railroad.
   D. To create a payment arrangement with the Central Pacific Railroad Company for the building of the railroad.

2. Which of the following reasons caused railroad construction to move slowly? Select ALL that apply.
   ☐ **1** The Sierra Nevada Mountains
   ☐ **2** Disagreements between the two railroad companies
   ☐ **3** Attacks from Native Americans
   ☐ **4** Bad weather
   ☐ **5** Not enough workers willing to do the dangerous work
   ☐ **6** Strikes by workers who wanted better pay
   ☐ **7** The Civil War

3. This question has two parts. First, answer Part A. Then, answer Part B.

Part A

Why were the two railroad companies in a rush to build the railroad as quickly as possible?

    A. Each company wanted to earn more money and land from the government.

    B. They were contractually obligated to finish the railroad by a certain date.

    C. They wanted to finish the railroad before the cold winter.

    D. They knew that the railroad was desperately needed by the American people.

Part B

What was the effect of the companies rushing to build the railroad?

    A. Some workers died due to the dangerous use of nitroglycerin.

    B. The railroad was completed much more quickly than expected.

    C. Some weak tracks had to be rebuilt later.

    D. Both A and C

4. Why did construction by the Central Pacific Railroad Company initially move slower than construction by the Union Pacific Railroad? Use evidence from the text to support your response.

_____

_____

_____

_____

_____

5. Why did railroad workers start using nitroglycerin, and what was the effect of this decision? Use evidence from the text to support your response.

_____

_____

_____

_____

_____

_____

6. Why did the two railroads meet in Promontory Summit?
   A. The two tracks coincidentally connected in Promontory Summit.
   B. President Ulysses Grant declared that the two tracks should meet in Promontory Summit.
   C. After being prompted by President Ulysses Grant, the two railroad companies decided to meet in Promontory Summit.
   D. Promontory Summit was the safest and most logical meeting place for the two railroads.

7. How did the transcontinental railroad make a positive impact on the United States? Use evidence from the text to support your answer.

_____

_____

_____

_____

_____

_____

8. How did the transcontinental railroad negatively impact the United States? Use evidence from the text to support your answer.

_____

_____

_____

_____

_____

_____

DETERMINE ACADEMIC AND DOMAIN-SPECIFIC WORD MEANING IN TEXT

RI.5.4 Determine the meaning of general academic and domain-specific words and phrases in a text relevant to a grade 5 topic or subject area.

Directions: Read the passage and answer the questions below.

Passage 1: Earth's Biomes *(Adapted from Encyclopaedia Britannica)*

1   Biomes, the major life zones of the continents, are defined by their plant communities. While animals are also important characteristics of biomes, vegetation is often an area's most apparent feature.

2   For these reasons, biomes are named for the most prominent type of vegetation they contain. Examples of biomes include forests and grasslands. In the world, there are six different types of biomes, some of which can be found in a variety of places. The six biomes are tundra, taiga, temperate deciduous forest, tropical rain forest, grassland and savanna, and desert. Let's take a look!

Tundra

3   The tundra biome is the coldest of the six biomes, so it's found only in extreme northern regions. It's so cold that underneath the layer of rocky topsoil, there's a permanently frozen layer of soil. This frozen soil makes it difficult for plants to flourish, so tundra is treeless land. With the exception of low vegetation such as lichens and mosses, there's very little plant life.

4   The two major tundra zones are the arctic tundra, located mostly north of the Arctic Circle, and the alpine tundra, found on tall mountains. Common tundra animals include reindeer and arctic foxes.

Taiga

5   The taiga, also known as the boreal forest, covers a broad region of land south of the tundra. It extends across the northern parts of Europe, Asia, and North America.

6   The taiga receives more rainfall than the tundra, especially in the summer months, and it's also warmer. Its vegetation consists mostly of evergreen trees, such as spruces and pines. Animals include moose, wolves, reindeer, bears, rabbits, and squirrels who have adapted to the cold and wet conditions.

Temperate Deciduous Forest

7 Temperate deciduous forests are located primarily in eastern North America, eastern Asia, and western Europe. These areas have frosty winters and moist, warm summers.

8 These forests consist mostly of hardwood trees with broad leaves. In the fall, these trees lose their leaves before growing new ones in the spring. Animals such as squirrels, rabbits, deer, wolves, bears, and birds inhabit this biome.

Tropical Rain Forest

9 Tropical rain forests are found in warm, wet areas near the equator. They have evergreen trees and many different plants and animals.

10 Rain forests have warm temperatures year-round and receive the most rainfall of any biome. The dense, upper layer of trees in the rain forest is called the canopy. The canopy is home to many animals who rarely venture from this layer. Air plants known as epiphytes, including orchids, ferns and bromeliads, live on tree trunks or branches.

11 Rainforest animals include gorillas and orangutans. Many of the animals found in this biome can't be found anywhere else on the planet.

Grassland and Savanna

12 Grasslands are found in temperate areas with little rainfall. They have few trees and shrubs, but contain a plethora of grasses. This biome extends across large parts of central North America and southern Africa. Grasslands have hot, dry summers and cold, damp winters.

13 Grasslands found in tropical areas are called savannas. Savannas have scattered trees that don't need much water to survive. They can be found in northern Australia, southern India and parts of Africa. They're warm year-round, with both wet and dry seasons.

Desert

14 Deserts are known for being extremely dry, and they typically receive less than 10 inches of rain annually. They usually contain very little vegetation. Plants and animals who live in the desert have adapted to surviving with hardly any water.

15 Common desert animals include lizards, snakes, mice, gophers, coyotes, foxes, and owls. To avoid daytime heat, many desert animals are nocturnal.

1. Based on the text, which of the following is the most *accurate* definition of a **biome?**
    - **A.** Six different types of land found in various continents or regions
    - **B.** Geographical areas that may be hot, cold, wet, or dry
    - **C.** A natural environment characterized by certain plants, animals, and climate
    - **D.** A scientific way to divide and categorize Earth's surface

2. Based on the sentence below, which of the following is the best definition of **flourish?**
   *This frozen soil makes it difficult for plants to **flourish,** so tundra is treeless land.*
   (Paragraph 3)
   - **A.** Receive sunlight
   - **B.** Grow
   - **C.** Exist
   - **D.** Spread

3. Based on the following sentence, which of the following is the best definition of **lichen?**
   *With the exception of low vegetation such as **lichens** and mosses, there's very little plant life. (Paragraph 3)*
   - **A.** A skin disease in which small bumps occur close together
   - **B.** A slow-growing plant that typically forms a growth on rocks, walls, and trees
   - **C.** A giant conifer with thick, fibrous bark that is noted for its great height
   - **D.** A shrub or clump of shrubs with stems of moderate length

4. Based on the following sentence, which of the following is the best definition of **inhabit?**
   *Animals such as squirrels, rabbits, deer, wolves, bears, and birds **inhabit** this biome.*
   (Paragraph 8)
   - **A.** Captivate
   - **B.** Endanger
   - **C.** Habitually
   - **D.** Occupy

5. Based on the following sentence, which of the following is the best definition for **venture?**
   *The canopy is home to many animals who rarely **venture** from this layer. (Paragraph 10)*
   - **A.** Arrive
   - **B.** Flee
   - **C.** Depart
   - **D.** Originate

6. Based on the following sentence, which of the following is the best definition of **plethora?**
   They have few trees and shrubs, but contain a plethora of grasses. (Paragraph 12)
   - **A.** Small amount
   - **B.** Large amount
   - **C.** Moderate amount
   - **D.** Lack of

7. Based on the sentence below, which of the following is the best definition for **annually?**
*Deserts are known for being extremely dry, and they typically receive less than 10 inches of rain **annually.** (Paragraph 14)*

    A. Weekly

    B. Daily

    C. Yearly

    D. Ever

8. Based on the information in Paragraph 15, how would you define the word **nocturnal?** What information in the passage helped you determine this definition?

_____

_____

_____

_____

_____

_____

_____

COMPARE & CONTRAST STRUCTURE OF EVENTS, IDEAS OR INFORMATION IN TEXTS

RI.5.5 Compare and contrast the overall structure (e.g., chronology, comparison, cause/effect, problem/solution) of events, ideas, concepts, or information in two or more texts.

Directions: Read the passage and answer the questions below.

Passage 1: Safety in Tornado Alley

1   If you live in the Midwest of the United States and you haven't seen a tornado before, it's likely that you will at some point in your life. The area is known as "tornado alley" because tornadoes occur there more often than in other areas in the U.S.

2   Tornados are one of the most violent types of severe weather. Characterized by extreme winds, tornadoes can cause significant property damage and even loss of life. Because of this, people living in tornado alley should put safety precautions in place to protect themselves and those they love when tornadoes come.

3   Storm shelters or safe rooms can give families living in tornado alley the protection of a room with walls that can withstand the dangerous high winds of the strongest tornadoes. People will often go to an interior room in their house, but the standard walls of a house cannot withstand the extreme winds and flying debris that a tornado can produce.

4   Because tornado storm shelters are built with reinforced steel or concrete and can be installed either in your yard or beneath your garage, you can know that your family will be safe if a tornado occurs.

1. This question has two parts. First, answer Part A. Then, answer Part B.

Part A
How is the text in Passage 1 organized?
- **A.** compare and contrast
- **B.** cause and effect
- **C.** chronological
- **D.** problem and solution

Part B

Describe how you know the text is organized by your answer to Part A. Use at least two details from the text to support your answer.

_____

_____

_____

_____

_____

_____

_____

2. Which detail would fit best after the first sentence in paragraph 2 in Passage 1?
   A. They are similar to hurricanes.
   B. They are caused by a combination of warm and cold air.
   C. I've seen several of them myself.
   D. They're not as dangerous as hurricanes, however.

3. Why does the author of Passage 1 most likely include the information about the lack of safety in interior rooms in a house?
   A. to demonstrate the destructive nature of tornados
   B. to explain the increased safety that cellars provide
   C. to help convince the reader why a tornado shelter is necessary
   D. to make the reader understand the danger of tornadoes

4. Based on the structure of Passage 1, what was the author's most likely reason for writing it?
   A. to give people in tornado alley a solution for staying safe in tornados
   B. to give people information about the danger of tornadoes
   C. to show people how destructive tornadoes can be
   D. to demonstrate the cause of tornadoes

Passage 2: Tornados and Hurricanes

1   Tornados and hurricanes are two of the most severe types of storms, and they can both be deadly and costly when they occur. They're both caused by an instability in atmospheric conditions and both produce extreme winds, which can cause destruction.

2   Tornadoes form as a rotating column of air on land. Hurricanes, however, are cyclones that only form on water. While tornados are feared for their destructive winds, hurricanes cause a majority of their destruction through flooding when they make landfall.

5. This question has two parts. First, answer Part A. Then, answer Part B.

Part A

How is the text in Passage 2 organized?

      A. compare and contrast

      B. cause and effect

      C. chronological

      D. problem and solution

Part B

Describe how you know the text is organized by your answer to Part A. Use details from the text to support your answer.

_____

_____

_____

_____

_____

_____

_____

6. Based on the structure of Passage 2, what is the author's most likely reason for including the information about tornados and hurricanes being formed by an instability in atmospheric conditions?

      A. to describe the cause of the destruction of tornadoes and hurricanes

      B. to demonstrate a similarity between tornadoes and hurricanes through comparison

      C. to illustrate the destructive nature of these types of storms

      D. to show a contrast between tornadoes and hurricanes

7. Compare and contrast the overall structure of the two passages 'Safety in Tornado Alley' and 'Tornados and Hurricanes'.

_____

_____

_____

_____

_____

_____

_____

8. Which of the following pieces of information do both passages share?

    A. Tornadoes are rotating columns of air.

    B. Tornadoes are caused by an instability in atmospheric conditions.

    C. Tornadoes produce destructive winds.

    D. Hurricanes produce flooding.

ANALYZE & COMPARE/CONTRAST MULTIPLE ACCOUNTS OF SAME TOPIC

RI.5.6 Analyze multiple accounts of the same event or topic, noting important similarities and differences in the point of view they represent.

Directions: Read the passage and answer the questions below.

Passage 1: Dangerous Pit Bulls

1   Pit bulls, a designation for several types of dogs with similar features, including the American Pit Bull Terrier, are some of the most dangerous dogs in the world. Known for their aggressive nature, pit bulls have developed a reputation for being excessively aggressive. They have been reported to attack people, including small children, causing serious harm and, in some cases, death.

2   Despite the danger, many families still choose to buy pit bulls as family pets, putting their family members at risk of attack. Of course, some pit bull advocates argue that pit bulls aren't inherently dangerous. Their behavior around people, they say, is largely influenced by how they are raised. The owners, they claim, are to blame if a pit bull chooses to be aggressive with a human being.

3   Regardless of what causes pit bulls to attack, research shows that pit bull attacks make up a majority of dog attacks in America. If owners are to blame for their aggressive behavior, then it would seem that people in general aren't responsible enough to own pit bulls.

1. Why did the author most likely write Passage 1?
    A. give the reader general information about pit bulls
    B. entertain the reader by giving funny stories about pit bulls
    C. convince the reader that pit bulls are dangerous
    D. reflect on the author's experience of owning a pit bull

2. After reading Passage 1, you can infer that the author
    A. has had a bad experience with pit bulls.
    B. thinks negatively about pit bulls.
    C. wishes more people would buy pit bulls.
    D. knows someone who owns a pit bull.

3. From what point-of-view is Passage 1 written?
    A. a first-person account of a pit bull victim
    B. a first-person account of a pit bull owner
    C. a third-person account of a pit bull owner
    D. a third-person account of a pit bull skeptic

Passage 2: My Pet Pit Bull

1   I got my pit bull, Molly, when I was eight years old, and she's been my best friend ever since then. I remember when my parents were looking at pets at the pet store. Molly stood out immediately, and I just stared at her through the glass. I begged my parents to buy her, but they almost didn't. Another customer, seeing my enthusiasm, suggested to my parents that pit bulls probably weren't the best choice for a family pet. They're aggressive and dangerous to children, the customer said.

2   Thankfully, my parents had done their research on pit bulls before bringing me to the store. It's true that pit bulls can be more aggressive than other dogs. They're not, however, inherently dangerous. When raised in a loving environment, pit bulls can be the best of companions. They're loyal and, rather than being a danger to their owners, they tend to be protective. However, they won't attack without being provoked.

3   Ever since that day in the pet store, I've wanted to help change the negative reputation of pit bulls. Pit bulls can be aggressive, and there have been reports of them attacking people, but these attacks aren't as prevalent as most people are led to believe. Instead of seeing that the majority of pit bull owners have raised dogs that are safe to be around, people often choose to highlight the rare occasions that pit bulls have attacked people.

4   The negative reputation of pit bulls is unfortunate and needs to change.

4. Why did the author most likely write Passage 2?
    A. to entertain the reader with a personal story about pit bulls
    B. to reflect on the author's experience of buying her first pit bull
    C. to provide information about why pit bulls are considered dangerous
    D. to convince the reader to reconsider the negative reputation of pit bulls

5. Which of the following quotes BEST supports the author's idea that pit bulls have been misunderstood?
    A. "I got my pit bull, Molly, when I was eight years old, and she's been my best friend ever since then." (Paragraph 1)
    B. "Another customer, seeing my enthusiasm, suggested to my parents that pit bulls probably weren't the best choice for a family pet." (Paragraph 1)
    C. "It's true that pit bulls can be more aggressive than other dogs." (Paragraph 2)
    D. "Pit bulls can be aggressive, and there have been reports of them attacking people, but these attacks aren't as prevalent as most people are led to believe." (Paragraph 3)

6. Which of the following is something both passages have in common?

    A. a love for pit bulls

    B. an acknowledgment of the aggressive nature of pit bulls

    C. an experience with owning a pit bull

    D. a discouraging from owning pit bulls

7. Which of the following quotes from Passage 2 would the author of Passage 1 be most likely to agree with?

    A. "It's true that pit bulls can be more aggressive than other dogs." (Paragraph 2)

    B. "When raised in a loving environment, pit bulls can be the best of companions." (Paragraph 2)

    C. "However, they won't attack without being provoked" (Paragraph 2)

    D. "The negative reputation of pit bulls is unfortunate and needs to change." (Paragraph 4)

8. Why do you think the authors describe pit bulls differently? Use details from the text to support your answer.

_____

_____

_____

_____

_____

_____

EXPLAIN HOW AUTHORS USE EVIDENCE TO SUPPORT POINTS OF VIEW

RI.5.8 Explain how an author uses reasons and evidence to support particular points in a text, identifying which reasons and evidence support which point(s).

Directions: Read the passage and answer the questions below.

Passage 1: Dr. Seuss

1   Dr. Seuss became one of the most well-known writers of children's books, creating stories that were fun and had a lyrical quality to them. Many adults remember reading classic Dr. Seuss stories, such as *The Cat in the Hat* and *Hop on Pop.* Seuss's stories have even become popular through film with Hollywood adaptations of *The Lorax* and *How the Grinch Stole Christmas.* Though he's known as a pioneer of entertaining children's stories, it was Dr. Seus's desire to see children becoming readers that most inspired him.

2   Dr. Seuss, whose real name was Theodor Seuss Geisel, was born on March 2, 1904 in Springfield, Massachusetts. He began his career as an illustrator and cartoonist. His artwork earned him a job drawing illustrations for product advertisements, and he was very successful doing so. He also created political cartoons and even worked in the animation department for the United States Army during World War II. During this time, he helped make a short documentary film that won the Academy Award for Best Documentary Feature in 1947.

3   It might have seemed that Dr. Seuss had found his career path in illustrating and cartooning, but after World War II, Geisel felt pulled toward writing books for children. Geisel began focusing on writing and illustrating his own children's books and adopted the name for which he is known, Dr. Seuss. He published books such as *If I Ran the Zoo* and *Horton Hears a Who!* The book and character he is perhaps most known for, however, is *The Cat in the Hat.*

4   *The Cat in the Hat,* a story about a mischievous cat who creates quite a mess with two young children in his quest for just a little fun, was written in response to a debate about children's literacy in the 1950s. After an author named John Hersey criticized the kinds of books children were exposed to in American schools, Dr. Seuss was given a list of words that all children should know and was challenged to write an entertaining and educational book with those words.

5   *The Cat in the Hat* was immediately well-received and inspired many children to read. As demonstrated in many of the other stories written by Dr. Seuss, Seuss's style of telling stories in whimsical rhymes with fun illustrations made reading enjoyable again for many children. Seuss went on to write many more books for children that were just as loved.

6   Ironically, though Dr. Seuss's career focused primarily on writing for children, for most of the time he was writing, Dr. Seuss didn't have any children of his own. When asked how he could

write stories that connected so well with children, Dr. Seuss once said, "You make 'em. I'll amuse 'em." It is interesting to note that Dr. Seuss wrote his first children's book the same year that he found out his wife, Helen, could not have children. Perhaps Dr. Seuss wrote for children to help fill a void in his own life.

7   The legacy of Dr. Seuss lives on as the popularity of his books continues among children today. The National Education Association even named Dr. Seuss's birthday, March 2, as National Read Across America Day each year, a day for people across America to celebrate literacy and Dr. Seuss's legacy.

1. This question has two parts. First, answer Part A. Then, answer Part B.

Part A
What is the author's message?
   A. Dr. Seuss began his career as an illustrator and cartoonist
   B. The Cat in the Hat is Dr. Seuss's most famous book
   C. Dr. Seuss was responsible for inspiring many children to become readers
   D. Dr. Seuss wrote primarily to entertain people

Part B
Which quote from the text best supports your answer in Part A?
   A. "He began his career as an illustrator and cartoonist, drawing illustrations for advertisements and even creating political cartoons." (Paragraph 2)
   B. "The Cat in the Hat was immediately well-received and inspired many children to read." (Paragraph 5)
   C. "Dr. Seuss became one of the most well-known writers of children's books, creating stories that were fun and had a lyrical quality to them." (Paragraph 1)
   D. "Though he's known as a pioneer of entertaining children's stories, it was his desire to see children becoming readers that most inspired him." (Paragraph 1)

2. Which quote from the text is used as evidence that Dr. Seuss wrote to both educate and entertain?
   A. "Seuss was given a list of words that all children should know and challenged to write an entertaining and educational book with those words." (Paragraph 4)
   B. "The Cat in the Hat was immediately well-received and inspired many children to read." (Paragraph 5)
   C. "Dr. Seuss became one of the most well-known writers of children's books, creating stories that were fun and had a lyrical quality to them." (Paragraph 1)
   D. "Dr. Seuss's style of telling stories in whimsical rhymes with fun illustrations made reading enjoyable again for many children." (Paragraph 5)

3. Which quote from the text contains the author's opinion?

    A. "He began his career as an illustrator and cartoonist, drawing illustrations for advertisements and even creating political cartoons." (Paragraph 2)

    B. "Seuss was given a list of words that all children should know and challenged to write an entertaining and educational book with those words." (Paragraph 4)

    C. "Seuss's stories have even become popular through film with Hollywood adaptations of The Lorax and How the Grinch Stole Christmas." (Paragraph 1)

    D. "The book and character he is perhaps most known for, however, is The Cat in the Hat." (Paragraph 3)

4. Read this sentence from paragraph 5:

    Dr. Seuss's style of telling stories in whimsical rhymes with fun illustrations made reading enjoyable again for many children.

Which point in the passage does this detail best support?

    A. Dr. Seuss's stories remain popular today.

    B. Dr. Seuss's books encouraged more reading among children.

    C. Dr. Seuss was probably most well-known as the author of The Cat in the Hat.

    D. Though he loved to draw, writing was what Dr. Seuss loved most.

5. This question has two parts. First, answer Part A. Then, answer Part B.

Part A

If Dr. Seuss hadn't become an author, what career might he have chosen?

    A. teacher

    B. songwriter

    C. politician

    D. illustrator/cartoonist

Part B

Which quote from the text best supports your answer in Part A?

    A. "Though he's known as a pioneer of entertaining children's stories, it was his desire to see children becoming readers that most inspired him." (Paragraph 1)

    B. "It might have seemed that Dr. Seuss had found his career path in illustrating advertising, but after World War II, Geisel felt pulled toward writing books for children." (Paragraph 3)

    C. "He also created political cartoons and even worked in the animation department for the United States Army during World War II." (Paragraph 3)

    D. "Dr. Seuss became one of the most well-known writers of children's books, creating stories that were fun and had a lyrical quality to them." (Paragraph 1)

6. What reason does the author give for why Dr. Seuss wrote for children and what evidence is given to support that reason?

_____

_____

_____

_____

_____

7. The passage proposes that Dr. Seuss's writing style helped to make his books so enjoyable for children. Select two quotes that support this point.

_____

_____

_____

_____

_____

8. Why do you think the author provides evidence that Dr. Seuss continues to have an impact on children today?

_____

_____

_____

_____

_____

INTEGRATE & EXPLAIN INFORMATION FROM SEVERAL TEXTS

RI.5.9 Integrate information from several texts on the same topic in order to write or speak about the subject knowledgeably.

Directions: Read the passage and answer the questions below.

Passage 1: Dr. King's Dream

1   Dr. Martin Luther King, Jr., who was born on January 15, 1929 in Atlanta, Georgia, was a civil rights leader and a pastor, who helped Americans see the injustice of segregation. During the time that King was growing up in America and well into his adulthood, segregation restricted African Americans like himself from going anywhere or participating in anything that was designated for white Americans only.

2   King was a minister, and he was inspired by the Bible's teaching on human equality. He was also moved by the ideas of the founding fathers, who made no differentiation in the Constitution or the Declaration of Independence about who should be guaranteed the "unalienable rights" of "life, liberty, and the pursuit of happiness." King saw that America was built on the idea that all human beings, regardless of their skin color, were to be guaranteed the same rights. Because of this, King made it his mission to fight for an America where white and African Americans would be viewed as equal.

3   Sometimes this fight led to him being arrested, which might make people wonder what crimes he was willing to commit to fight for freedom. King was committed to the idea of peaceful protest, however. In fact, in his famous "I Have a Dream" speech, he urged his fellow African Americans to refuse to fight injustice with violence.

4   King's commitment to equality helped to end racial segregation in America, making at least a part of his "dream" a reality.

1. Which of the following is the main idea of Passage 1?
   A. Dr. Martin Luther King, Jr. spoke eloquently about segregation and was arrested as a result.
   B. Dr. Martin Luther King, Jr. was a civil rights leader who peacefully fought for equal rights for African Americans.
   C. Segregation was a serious problem in Dr. Martin Luther King, Jr.'s time, but his efforts put an end to it.
   D. Dr. Martin Luther King, Jr. once gave a speech called "I Have a Dream" about how he wanted to end segregation.

2. This question has two parts. First, answer Part A. Then, answer Part B.

Part A

Which of the following did NOT motivate Dr. King's fight for equal rights?

    A. the Bible

    B. the Constitution and the Declaration of Independence

    C. segregation

    D. violent protest

Part B

Which of the following quotes best supports your answer to Part A?

    A. "During the time that King was growing up in America and well into his adulthood, segregation restricted African Americans like himself from going anywhere or participating in anything that was designated for white Americans only." (Paragraph 1)

    B. "King saw that America was built on the idea that all human beings, regardless of their skin color, were to be guaranteed the same rights." (Paragraph 2)

    C. "Sometimes this fight led to him being arrested, which might make people wonder what crimes he was willing to commit to fight for freedom." (Paragraph 3)

    D. "In fact, in his famous "I Have a Dream" speech, he urged his fellow African Americans to refuse to fight injustice with violence." (Paragraph 3)

Passage 2: Dr. King's Fight

1   You may not realize it, but there was a time in America's history when people of different races were segregated from one another. Segregation, which is defined as "setting something apart," meant that African American people weren't allowed to go anywhere they wanted in America or participate in any activity they wanted. For example, in some places in America, if you wanted to ride the bus to travel from one place to another, you couldn't sit in the front of the bus if you were an African American. Some water fountains were designated white-only. These are only two examples of the segregation African Americans faced every day in America.

2   While racism still exists in America today, segregation is a thing of the past, thanks to the Civil Rights Movement of the 1950s and 1960s. The most well-known figure of the Civil Rights Movement was an African American pastor named Dr. Martin Luther King, Jr.

3   Growing up as an African American man, surrounded by racial injustice everywhere he looked, King was driven to change the way inequality was accepted as the status quo in America. Because he was a minister who believed in a God who creates all people equal, he felt a responsibility to his fellow African Americans to fight for equal rights.

4   In his fight for equality, Dr. King believed only in peaceful protest. He didn't believe violence would solve anything. Even though his protests were peaceful, Dr. King often found himself in trouble with the law. On October 19, 1960, Dr. King and several other African Americans were arrested in Atlanta, Georgia for refusing to leave their seats at a department store lunch counter. Because of segregation laws, African Americans were forbidden to be served at store lunch counters, and Dr. King saw this as an obvious injustice. Whites and African Americans were only different in the color of their skin. Underneath, they were both human, deserving of the same rights. Dr. King's peaceful protest that day in 1960 landed him in a jail cell. He was freed by then Presidential candidate John F. Kennedy. Even though Dr. King faced unfair treatment, he never gave up his pursuit of equal rights for all Americans, regardless of their skin color.

5   Dr. King devoted his life to the battle for equality, and he ultimately gave his life for it. His life was tragically cut short when a man named James Earl Ray shot and killed Dr. King on April 4, 1968 in Memphis, Tennessee. His legacy continues to live on, however, in those who still believe in his dream that racism will one day end.

3. Which of the following is the main idea of Passage 2?
   - **A.** Dr. Martin Luther King, Jr. believed that violence would never help to gain African Americans their rights.
   - **B.** Dr. Martin Luther King, Jr. was once arrested for peacefully protesting against segregation in a department store lunch counter.
   - **C.** Even though segregation once kept African Americans from enjoying equality, Dr. Martin Luther King, Jr. gave his life to fighting peacefully for equal rights for African Americans.
   - **D.** James Earl Ray, who disagreed with Dr. Martin Luther King's fight for equality, shot and killed Dr. King on April 4, 1968.

4. After reading both passages, it can be inferred that Dr. Martin Luther King, Jr. was
    A. a violent protestor.
    B. a timid speaker.
    C. an angry tyrant.
    D. a compassionate leader.

5. What does the author of Passage 2 reveal about one of Dr. King's arrests that Passage 1 doesn't mention?
    A. his arrest was the result of refusing to leave an area reserved for whites only
    B. he fought back physically against his arrest
    C. he was released after a warning not to protest again
    D. he was killed shortly after

6. Based on both passages, how old was Dr. King when he died?
    A. 29
    B. 37
    C. 40
    D. 39

7. Read the following sentence from Passage 1.
    King was a minister, and he was inspired by the Bible's teaching on human equality.
    Which of the following quotes from Passage 2 most closely communicates the same idea?
    A. "Because he was a minister who believed in a God who creates all people equal, he felt a responsibility to his fellow African Americans to fight for equal rights." (Paragraph 3)
    B. "In his fight for equality, Dr. King believed only in peaceful protest." (Paragraph 4)
    C. "Underneath, they were both human, deserving of the same rights." (Paragraph 4)
    D. "Dr. King devoted his life to the battle for equality, and he ultimately gave his life for it." (Paragraph 5)

8. What important details does Passage 2 include that are absent from Passage 1.

_____

_____

_____

_____

_____

LANGUAGE

HAVE COMMAND OF GRAMMAR & USAGE

L.5.1   Demonstrate command of the conventions of standard English grammar and usage when writing or speaking.

Understand Conjunctions, Prepositions, and Interjections

L.5.1A Explain the function of conjunctions, prepositions, and interjections in general and their function in particular sentences.

1. Identify the interjection in the sentence below.
    Stop! You don't want to get hit by that car!
A. Stop!	**B.** You don't
C. get hit	**D.** car

2. Identify the preposition in the following sentence.
    When my mom called, I was with my friends.
A. when	**B.** my mom
C. with	**D.** my friends

3. Complete the following sentence by choosing the BEST preposition.
    Charlie was surprised to see the remote-control firetruck zooming _____ the floor.
A. from	**B.** across
C. under	**D.** near

4. Read the following sentence and underline the conjunction. Then revise it by placing a comma in the correct place.
    Jonathan's uncle has been looking for a job but he is still able to pay his bills from his savings account.

    _____

    _____

Form and Use Perfect Verb Tenses

L.5.1B Form and use the perfect (e.g. I had walked; I have walked; I will have walked) verb tenses.

1. Which verb tense is being used in the following sentence?
    Daveed will have finished his essay by the time it is due to his teacher.
A. past perfect tense	**B.** present perfect tense
C. future perfect tense	**D.** past progressive tense

2. Complete the following sentence with the correct form of the verb.

   I _____ pulled the car into the garage last night, since it is snowing today.

   A. would have   **B.** should have
   C. had   **D.** might have

3. Which sentence correctly revises the sentence below by using present **perfect verb tense?**
   Scarlett played basketball for four seasons.

   A. Scarlett had played basketball for four seasons.
   B. Scarlett has played basketball for four seasons.
   C. Scarlett will have played basketball for four seasons.
   D. Scarlett have played basketball for four seasons.

4. Complete the chart with sentences that use the appropriate perfect verb tenses for the verb *run.*

Verb Tense	Sentence
Perfect	
present perfect	
past perfect	

Use Verb Tense to Convey Time, Sequences, States and Conditions
L.5.1C Use verb tense to convey various times, sequences, states, and conditions.

1. Which sentence correctly uses a verb in the past tense?
   A. The marching band won first place in their competition.
   B. The marching band will compete in several other parades.
   C. The marching band is going to Disney World this week.
   D. The marching band practices up to three times a week.

2. Read the following sentence. Then identify the revised sentence that uses the verb in future tense.
   After school, Kacey walked home from the bus stop before doing her homework.

   A. After school, Kacey walks home from the bus stop before doing her homework.
   B. After school, Kacey will walk home from the bus stop before doing her homework.
   C. Before school, Kacey walked home from the bus stop before doing her homework.
   D. After school, Kacey is walking home from the bus stop before she will do her homework.

3. Identify the sentence written in present tense.
   A. David will make a cake for his mother's birthday.
   B. Johanna went to her cousin's housewarming party.
   C. Shortly, Rex will compete in the BMX race.
   D. We are all excited about the holiday season.

4. Write a paragraph of at least three sentences that describes what you did at school yesterday, what you are doing today, and what you hope to do tomorrow. Use the correct verb tense for each description.

_____

_____

_____

_____

Understand Shifts in Verb Tense

L.5.1D Recognize and correct inappropriate shifts in verb tense.

1. Which sentence correctly uses appropriate verb tense?
   A. The boy sprinted to the mailbox and checks the mail.
   B. The boy sprinted to the mailbox and checking the mail.
   C. The boy sprinted to the mailbox and checked the mail.
   D. The boy sprinted to the mailbox and check the mail.

2. This is a two-part question. First answer Part A, then Part B.

Part A

Read the following sentence and identify the revision that demonstrates correct usage of the verbs in the sentence.

Last week, Jules played baseball in a scrimmage and was scoring a run.
   A. Last week, Jules plays baseball in a scrimmage and was scoring a run.
   B. Last week, Jules played baseball in a scrimmage and score a run.
   C. Last week, Jules will play baseball in a scrimmage and scored a run.
   D. Last week, Jules played baseball in a scrimmage and scored a run.

Part B

What context clue from the sentence in Part A helps the reader determine the appropriate verb tense?
   A. Last week   **B.** baseball
   C. In a scrimmage   **D.** was scoring

3. Read the following sentence. Revise the underlined word using appropriate verb tense.

   By the time the music began, most of the crowd <u>have left </u>the concert hall.

       A. will leave   **B.** had left

       C. left   **D.** had leaved

4. Read the following paragraph. It contains many incorrect shifts in verb tense. Revise the passage by correcting the errors.

   Once upon a time, there is a girl who loved to spend summers at swim camp. There, she did many of her favorite things. She play water polo. She will go swimming. She got to hang out with some of her best friends. She make many friendships at swim camp and can't wait to go back!

   _____

   _____

   _____

   _____

Use Correlative Conjunctions

L.5.1E Use correlative conjunctions (e.g., either/or, neither/nor).

1. Select the best pair of correlative conjunctions to complete the following sentence:

   _____ *had I walked in the door* _____ *my phone began to ring.*

       A. Either/ or   **B.** Both/ and

       C. No sooner/ than   **D.** Neither/ nor

2. Identify the correlative conjunctions used in the sentence.

   Pamela is not only good at baseball, but she's also an excellent musician.

       A. not only/ but also   **B.** not/ only

       C. is/ also   **D.** only good/ also

3. Write two sentences using the different correlative conjunctions in the chart.

Correlative Conjunctions	Sentence
either, or	
neither, nor	

4. Combine the following two sentences with correlative conjunctions.

   Dayton does not like carrots. Juliana does not like carrots either.

   _____

   _____

KNOW CAPITALIZATION, PUNCTUATION, & SPELLING

L.5.2 Demonstrate command of the conventions of standard English capitalization, punctuation, and spelling when writing.

Use Punctuation to Separate Items

L.5.2A Use punctuation to separate items in a series.

1. Which sentence shows the correct way to use commas to punctuate separate items in a series?
   - **A.** Please clean your room, do the dishes, take out the trash, and do your homework before you watch tv.
   - **B.** Please, clean your room do the dishes, take out the trash and do your homework before you watch tv.
   - **C.** Please clean your room, do the dishes, take out the trash, and do your homework before, you watch tv.
   - **D.** Please clean your room do the dishes take out the trash, and do your homework before you watch tv.

2. Complete the chart below by adding commas to show correct punctuation for each series.

Series	Series with Punctuation
wake up brush my teeth eat breakfast and catch the bus	
Jessica Lori Pam and Jasmine	
chicken green beans potatoes and sweet tea	

3. Identify the word in the sentence that needs a comma after it.
   Our candy bar consists of popcorn, Gummy Bears, Skittles and chocolate chips in small bowls on the counter.
   - **A.** bar,
   - **B.** Skittles,
   - **C.** in,
   - **D.** bowls,

4. Rewrite the following sentence with correct punctuation.
   Our basketball uniform consists of a shirt shorts socks and a sweatband.

_____

_____

Use Commas to Separate Introductions

L.5.2B Use a comma to separate an introductory element from the rest of the sentence.

1. Which sentence shows the correct way to use commas to separate an introductory phrase?
    A. At the movies, I will buy popcorn.
    B. I will buy popcorn, candy, and a soda at the movies.
    C. Jamie will visit with his dad, his cousins, and his mom.
    D. Jesse's brother, who likes to dance, is hosting a party.

2. Read the following sentence. Identify the word that should have a comma after it.
When it is time for school to start the bell will ring.
    A. time,
    B. school,
    C. start,
    D. bell,

3. Which sentence correctly uses a comma after an introductory phrase?
    A. After, being stung by a bee Sam cried for an hour.
    B. On her birthday Juana, got a cat.
    C. While eating dinner, the family shared about their day.
    D. If she wants to get good grades she needs to study.

4. Write a sentence using the introductory phrase "in summary" and correctly use a comma.

_____

_____

_____

_____

Use Commas for Tag Questions and Indirect Address

L.5.2C Use a comma to set off the words yes and no (e.g., Yes, thank you), to set off a tag question from the rest of the sentence (e.g., It's true, isn't it?), and to indicate direct address (e.g., Is that you, Steve?).

1. Which sentence has the correct punctuation?
    A. No I don't need a ride.
    B. Is that you John?
    C. Yes, I do need a ruler.
    D. It's true isn't it?

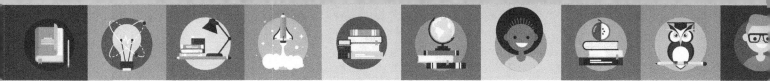

2. How should the following sentence be punctuated to offset the tag words?

Please open the window so that we don't suffocate in here.

    A. Please open the window so that we don't suffocate, in here.

    B. Please, open the window so that we don't suffocate in here.

    C. Please open, the window so that we don't suffocate in here.

    D. Please open the window so, that we don't suffocate in here.

3. Read the following sentence, then add a logical question tag at the end.

They won't cheat, _____ .

_____

_____

_____

_____

4. Determine the correct tag question for the following phrase:

You brought your coat,

    A. won't you?

    B. didn't you?

    C. can't you?

    D. didn't they?

Use Correct Grammar to Indicate Titles of Works

L.5.2D Use underlining, quotation marks, or italics to indicate titles of works.

1. Which sentence correctly notates the title of a book?

    A. I read <u>the book Holes</u> with my class.

    B. Eli recommended that I read the book <u>Wonder.</u>

    C. Have you read the book "Huckleberry Finn?"

    D. The book The Jungle Book is my favorite.

2. Which is the right way to write the article title How to Baste a Turkey.

    A. "How to Baste a Turkey"

    B. <u>How to Baste a Turkey</u>

    C. *How to Baste a Turkey*

    D. How To Baste A "Turkey"

3. Choose the correct way to write the short story title Rapunzel.

    A. *Rapunzel*   **B.** **"Rapunzel"**

    C. <u>Rapunzel</u>   **D.** Rapunzel

4. Revise the following sentence to use correct naming conventions.

When I was younger, my favorite book was Corduroy, but now that I'm older, I prefer the book Bridge To Terabithia.

_____

_____

Spell Correctly

L.5.2E Spell grade-appropriate words correctly, consulting references as needed.

1. Which sentence contains a misspelled word?
    A. The teacher provided an introduction to the Social Studies chapter.
    B. Tomorrow our glass will give our habitat presentashun.
    C. I'm concerned with the amount of deception and cheating in high school.
    D. I'd like to present my visual representation of the planets.

2. Which sentence includes the correct use of a homophone?
    A. The boy pushed his bicycle's <u>break</u> to stop.
    B. I was so <u>board</u> the day I have to go to my dad's office.
    C. I'm ready to <u>bored</u> the bus.
    D. I <u>sent</u> a very enthusiastic letter to the principal.

3. Read the following sentence and correct the underlined word.
    A <u>sell</u> is the smallest part of a living thing.
    A. scell   B. cell
    C. sell   D. celle

4. Read the following dictionary definitions of homophones 'creak' and 'creek'. Then use both words in a sentence or sentences, using each word's correct spelling and meaning.
    creak
    1. (verb) a high-pitched sound, often from movement due to pressure or weight
    2. (noun) a harsh scraping or squeaking sound
    creek
    1. (noun) a streak, brook, or small offshoot of a river
    2. (noun) an inlet in a shoreline or other sheltered waterway

_____

_____

UNDERSTAND & USE APPROPRIATE LANGUAGE CONVENTIONS

L.5.3 Use knowledge of language and its conventions when writing, speaking, reading, or listening.

Expand, Combine, and Reduce Sentences

L.5.3A   Expand, combine, and reduce sentences for meaning, reader/listener interest, and style.

1. Read the sentence below. Then choose the revision that makes the sentence more effective and powerful.

    Bradley waited for his lunch.

    A. Bradley waited for lunch.

    B. Bradley eagerly waited for the delectable lunch.

    C. Bradley wondered where his lunch was.

    D. Bradly helplessly waited for his speedy lunch.

2. Use a conjunction to effectively combine the following sentences.

    Joe wanted to play hockey. Joe couldn't skate very well.

    _____

    _____

    _____

3. Read the following sentence. Then choose the revision that reduces the sentence to make it more powerful.

    James really likes BMX biking, because it is exciting—more exciting than any other sport he knows about.

    A. James loves BMX biking because he thinks it's the most exciting sport.

    B. James sort of likes BMX biking because he thinks it is more exciting that other sports he knows about.

    C. James thinks BMX biking is the best sport because out of all the sports it is exciting.

    D. James really likes BMX biking and it's the most exciting sport.

4. Choose the BEST conjunction to combine the following sentences.

    The children are afraid of the storm. Their mother let them sleep on her floor.

    A. but   **B.** because

    C. and   **D.** so

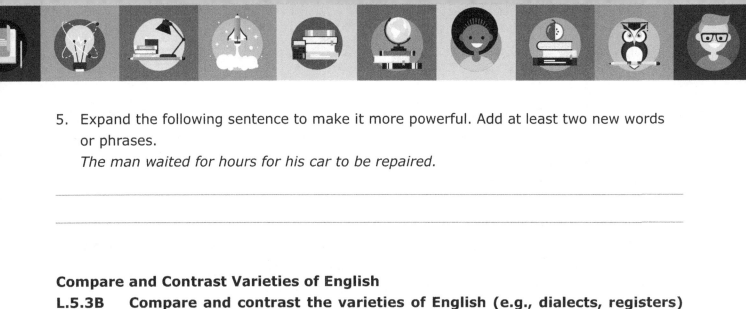

5. Expand the following sentence to make it more powerful. Add at least two new words or phrases.
   The man waited for hours for his car to be repaired.

_____

_____

Compare and Contrast Varieties of English

L.5.3B   Compare and contrast the varieties of English (e.g., dialects, registers) used in stories, dramas, or poems.

1. The variety of language that a group of people speak is known as
   A. register
   B. formal speech
   C. informal speech
   D. dialect

2. Read the following sentence written in American Southern dialect. Then identify its meaning.
   "Ya'll ain't gonna believe what I can do!"
   A. You will believe what I can do!
   B. You all are not going to believe what I can do!
   C. You'll are gonna believe what I can do!
   D. You're aren't going to believe what I can do!

3. Read the following excerpt from *Holes* by Louis Sachar.
   Squid returned with four other boys. The first three were introduced by Mr. Pendanski as José, Theodore, and Ricky. They called themselves Magnet, Armpit, and Zigzag.

   "They all have nicknames," explained Mr. Pendanski. "However, I prefer to use the names that their parents gave them—the names that *society will recognize them* by when they return to become useful and hardworking members of society."

   What register does Mr. Pendanski use?
   A. informal
   B. casual
   C. formal
   D. excited

4. Read the following statement written in an informal register. Rewrite it using a formal register.
   Hey. What're you doing tonight? I'm thinking about hanging out with some friends and grabbing a bite to eat. You in?

_____

_____

_____

LANGUAGE

5. Read the following dialogue from *Huck Finn* by Mark Twain.

   Jim: "We's safe, Huck, we's safe! Jump up and crack yo' heels. Dat's de good ole Cairo at las', I jis knows it."

   Huck: "I'll take the canoe and go see, Jim. It mightn't be, you know."

   How does Twain use dialect?

   A. He uses dialect to develop characters, especially Jim as a southern commoner.

   B. He uses dialect to show that Huck is smarter than Jim.

   C. He uses dialect to develop the setting of the novel.

   D. He uses dialect to make the text more difficult for the reader.

DETERMINE MEANING OF UNKNOWN WORDS WHEN READING

L.5.4 Determine & clarify the meaning of unknown and multiple-meaning words and phrases based on reading.

Use Context Clues

L.5.4A Use context (e.g., cause/effect relationships and comparisons in text) as a clue to the meaning of a word or phrase.

Directions: Read the passage from Little Women *by Louisa May Alcott then answer questions 1 -4.*

1   "Merry Christmas, little daughters! But I want to say one word before we sit down. Not far away from here lies a poor woman with a little newborn baby. Six children are huddled into one bed to keep from freezing, for they have no fire. There is nothing to eat over there, and the oldest boy came to tell me they were suffering hunger and cold. My girls, will you give them your breakfast as a Christmas present?"

2   They were all unusually hungry, having waited nearly an hour, and for a minute no one spoke, only a minute, for Jo exclaimed impetuously, "I'm so glad you came before we began!"

3   "May I go and help carry the things to the poor little children?" asked Beth eagerly.

4   "I shall take the cream and the muffins," added Amy, heroically giving up the article she most liked.

5   Meg was already covering the buckwheats, and piling the bread into one big plate.

6   "I thought you'd do it," said Mrs. March, smiling as if satisfied. "You shall all go and help me, and when we come back we will have bread and milk for breakfast, and make it up at dinnertime."

7   They were soon ready, and the procession set out. Fortunately it was early, and they went through back streets, so few people saw them, and no one laughed at the queer party.

8   A poor, bare, miserable room it was, with broken windows, no fire, ragged bedclothes, a sick mother, wailing baby, and a group of pale, hungry children cuddled under one old quilt, trying to keep warm.

9   How the big eyes stared and the blue lips smiled as the girls went in.

1. What is the meaning of the word *procession* as it is used in paragraph 7?
    A. march
    C. group walking
    B. demonstration
    D. celebratory parade

2. **Part A**

   What does the phrase *blue lips* imply, as it is used in paragraph 9?

   A. the children were starving

   B. the family was cold

   C. the children were shocked

   D. the entire family was sick

   Part B

   Which detail from the passage supports the answer to Part A?

   A. "children cuddled under one old quilt, trying to keep warm"

   B. "hungry children"

   C. "A poor, bare, miserable room it was"

   D. "no one laughed at the queer party"

3. Which context clue supports the meaning for the word *huddled* (paragraph 2) as crowded?

   A. "for they have no fire"

   B. "one bed"

   C. "nothing to eat over there"

   D. "they were suffering"

4. Reread the following sentence.

   Meg was already covering the buckwheats, and piling the bread into one big plate.

   Explain the meaning of the word "piling" in the context of this passage, and explain what context clues help you understand its meaning.

   _____

   _____

Use Greek and Latin Affixes and Roots

L.5.4B Use common, grade-appropriate Greek and Latin affixes and roots as clues to the meaning of a word (e.g., photograph, photosynthesis).

1. Read the following sentence.

   "A major export of China is electronics."

   The prefix "ex-" means "out of" or "away from." In this sentence the prefix "ex-" is added to the word "port", which changes its meaning. Which definition fits the word "export?"

   A. a good that comes in

   B. a good that is carried away

   C. a ship that carries goods

   D. Chinese money

2. Write the meaning of each root in the chart below. Then create a new word using the root and affix(es).

Root	Meaning	My Word
photo		
rupt		
script		
dict		

3. Read the sentence below. Fill in the appropriate root in the blank.

   The young woman's attempt to steal from the jewelry store were il_____.

   A. legible

   B. logical

   C. legal

   D. lustrated

4. Read the following sentence.

   Before the magician performed for the school assembly, the electrician attempted to fix the sound system.

   Using the context clues and your knowledge of affixes, explain the meaning of the suffix -ian in one sentence.

   _____

   _____

   _____

Use Reference Materials to Determine Meaning

L.5.4C Consult reference materials (e.g., dictionaries, glossaries, thesauruses), both print and digital, to find the pronunciation and determine or clarify the precise meaning of key words and phrases.

*Read this passage from **Across the Plains** by Robert Louis Stevenson.*

   I must tell here an experience of mine with another newsboy. I tell it because it gives so good an example of that uncivil kindness of the American, which is perhaps their most bewildering character to one newly landed. It was immediately after I had left the emigrant train; and I am told I looked like a man at death's door, so much had this long journey shaken me. I sat at the end of a car, and the catch being broken, and myself feverish and sick, had

to hold the door open with my foot for the sake of air. In this attitude my leg debarred the newsboy from his box of merchandise. I made haste to let him pass when I observed that he was coming; but I was busy with a book, and so once or twice he came upon me unawares. On these occasions he most rudely struck my foot aside; and though I myself apologised, as if to show him the way, he answered me never a word. I chafed furiously, and I fear the next time it would have come to words. But suddenly I felt a touch upon my shoulder, and a large juicy pear was put into my hand. It was the newsboy, who had observed that I was looking ill, and so made me this present out of a tender heart. For the rest of the journey I was petted like a sick child; he lent me newspapers, thus depriving himself of his legitimate profit on their sale, and came repeatedly to sit by me and cheer me up.

1. A student determines that the meaning of the word "uncivil" is rude. She knows that the prefix -un means "not." She has consulted a dictionary to find the definition of the word "civil." Which of the following definitions states the meaning of the word "civil" as it is used in the passage?
    A. adjective relating to ordinary citizens
    B. adjective relating to the law
    C. adjective courteous and polite
    D. adjective fixed by custom or law rather than being natural

2. The student has now consulted a thesaurus to find an exact synonym for the word "uncivil" as it is used in this excerpt. Which of the following is the BEST synonym for "uncivil"?
    A. not a citizen
    B. impolite
    C. unlawful
    D. unnatural

3. In this passage the newsboy is rude, but at the same time, he's kind and generous. Stevenson says his experience is an example of Americans' "most bewildering character." Look up the definition of the word "bewilder" in the dictionary to BEST explain its meaning in the context of this passage.

    _____

    _____

    _____

    _____

    _____

4. Read the three dictionary definitions for the word present.

   present

   adjective

   1. (of a person) in a particular place
   2. existing or occurring now

   noun

   3. the period of time now occurring
   4. a gift

   verb

   5. give something to someone
   6. bring about or be the cause of

Read the sentence, "It was the newsboy, who had observed that I was looking ill, and so made me this present out of a tender heart." Which part of speech and definition is used in this sentence?

   A. *adjective* (of a person) in a particular place
   B. *noun* the period of time now occurring
   C. *noun* a gift
   D. *verb* give something to someone

UNDERSTAND FIGURATIVE LANGUAGE & WORD RELATIONSHIPS

L.5.5 Demonstrate understanding of figurative language, word relationships, and nuances in word meanings.

Interpret Figurative Language

L.5.5A Interpret figurative language, including similes and metaphors, in context.

1. Read the following sentence and interpret the figurative language.

    "Writing that paper was a piece of cake! Since the book was so interesting, writing a paper was no problem at all."

    The phrase "piece of cake" means

    A. it was easy.

    B. it was tiring.

    C. I did it over dinner.

    D. the writer loves cake.

2. Read the following sentence, then determine the meaning of the underlined metaphor.

    At the crowded fair, I had trouble picking out my friends in the <u>sea of people.</u>

    A. water rides

    B. beach chairs

    C. busy crowd

    D. wall of people

3. Read the following sentence.

    "When my dad wakes up in the morning, he's a bear."

    What is being compared in the sentence? Explain what the writer might mean when she makes this comparison.

    _____

    _____

    _____

    _____

    _____

    _____

4. Rewrite the following sentence with a simile or metaphor.

   "The clouds in the sky were fluffy."

   _____

   _____

   _____

   _____

   _____

Recognize and Explain Idioms, Adages, and Proverbs
L.5.5B Recognize and explain the meaning of common idioms, adages, and proverbs.

1. Read the sentence. Then identify the correct meaning of the idiom used.

   "When the storm rolled in, we could hear the rain pelting the roof. 'It's <u>raining cats and dogs!</u>' my dad shouted."

   A. there is more wind than rain

   B. it's raining hard

   C. the storm will scare the animals

   D. the roof is in danger of collapsing

2. Choose the correct word to complete the adage below.

   "Don't judge a _____ by its cover."

   A. car

   B. speaker

   C. book

   D. person

3. Read the sentence containing an idiom below.

   "Last Halloween, my friend's father dressed up as a baby, using a diaper and a pacifier as props. When I saw him, I doubled over and died laughing."

   Which context clues help the reader understand the meaning of the idiom "died laughing?"

   A. Last Halloween

   B. when I saw

   C. father dressed up as a baby

   D. as props

4. Read the following passage, then explain the meaning of the underlined idioms and adages.
   "Jana was nervous as she took the stage—so nervous she couldn't shake the <u>butterflies in her stomach.</u> She looked around at her friends warming up in the wings. She <u>caught the eye</u> of her friend Sally. '<u>Break a leg,</u> Jana," Sally whispered."

   _____

   _____

   _____

   _____

   _____

   _____

Understand Word Relationships

L.5.5C Use the relationship between particular words (e.g., synonyms, antonyms, homographs) to better understand each of the words.

1. Read the following sentence. Then, replace the underlined word with a synonym.
   The girls <u>usually</u> go to the soda shop right after they get out of band rehearsal.
   - **A.** frequently
   - **B.** sometimes
   - **C.** always
   - **D.** occasionally

2. Read the following sentence. Then identify the correct meaning of the underlined homograph based on the context of the sentence.
   "We were going to play a mixed doubles tennis <u>match</u> today, but my partner came down with an illness."
   - **A.** a person able to contend with another as an equal
   - **B.** a contest in which people or teams compete
   - **C.** a slender piece of wood for lighting things on fire
   - **D.** to fit two things together

3. Read the following sentence.
   "The child became <u>irate</u> when his sister got the last piece of chocolate cake."
   Which of the following choices is NOT an appropriate synonym for the word irate?
   - **A.** upset
   - **B.** angry
   - **C.** furious
   - **D.** loud

4. Look at the graphic below. Each of the words in the outside triangles are antonyms to a missing word in the center. Fill in the center space with the antonym.

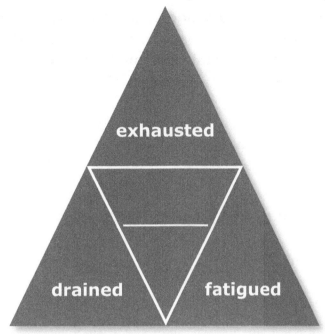

KNOW & USE GENERAL ACADEMIC/DOMAIN-SPECIFIC WORDS

L.5.6 Acquire and use accurately grade-appropriate general academic and domain-specific words and phrases, including those that signal contrast, addition, and other logical relationships (e.g., however, although, nevertheless, similarly, moreover, in addition).

Read the following poem "The Story of Fidgety Philip" by Dr. Henrich Hoffman. Then answer questions 1-4.

Passage 1: "The Story of Fidgety Philip" by Dr. Henrich Hoffman

1   Let me see if Philip can
Be a little gentleman
Let me see, if he is able
To sit still for once at table:
Thus Papa bade Phil behave;
And Mamma look'd very grave.

2   But fidgety Phil,
He won't sit still;
He wriggles
and giggles,
And then, I declare
Swings backwards and forwards
And tilts up his chair,
Just like any rocking horse; -
"Philip! I am getting cross!"

3   See the naughty restless child
Growing still more rude and wild.
Till his chair falls over quite.
Philip screams with all his might.
Catches at the cloth, but then
That makes matters worse again.
Down upon the ground they fall.
Glasses, plates, knives, forks and all.
How Mamma did fret and frown.

4   When she saw them tumbling down!
And Papa made such a face!
Philip is in sad disgrace.

5   Fairly cover'd up you see!
Cloth and all are lying on him;
He has pull'd down all upon him.
What a terrible to-do!
Dishes, glasses, snapt in two!
Here a knife, and there a fork!

6   Philip, this is cruel work.
Table all so bare, and ah!
Poor Papa, and poor Mamma
Look quite cross, and wonder how
They shall make their dinner now.

1. What does the word *grave* (stanza 1) mean in the context of this passage?
    - **A.** gracious
    - **B.** worried
    - **C.** crucial
    - **D.** stern

2. Which statement from the passage best supports the meaning of the word *fidgety?*
    - **A.** "He won't sit still"
    - **B.** "naughty"
    - **C.** "Be a little gentleman"
    - **D.** "cruel work"

3. Reread this phrase.
    "Thus Papa bade Phil behave"
    The word *bade* can be replaced with the word
    - **A.** wished
    - **B.** told
    - **C.** explained
    - **D.** couldn't

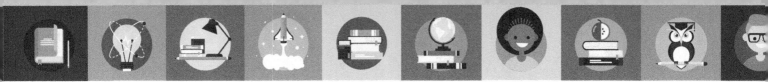

4. Write a definition for the word *disgrace* as it is used in the poem.

_____

_____

_____

_____

5. Read the following sentence. Which word BEST replaces the underlined word?
Only the hardiest crops can <u>resist </u>the harsh freezing conditions.
   A. survive
   B. grow
   C. cultivate
   D. parch

6. Read the following sentence. Which word BEST replaces the underlined word?
Our classroom has <u>sufficient </u>space to add the three new students.
   A. concentrated
   B. unnecessary
   C. adequate
   D. courteous

7. Read the following sentence. Which word signals a contrast between two things or ideas?
We asked for everyone to provide three supplies, however most participants only brought one.
   A. asked
   B. provide
   C. however
   D. only... one

8. Read the sentences below. Then determine what is being compared in the sentences due to the word "similarly."
The shoes are inexpensive, so more people can afford them. Similarly, the socks are also affordable.
   A. what people can afford
   B. the price of shoes and socks
   C. expensive and inexpensive items
   D. people and clothing

9. Fill in the blank with the appropriate word.

    _____ I was sick, I still had to take my math test.

    A. Because

    B. So

    C. However

    D. Although

10. Fill in the blank with the appropriate word.

    Workers _____ the Erie Canal to connect the Hudson River to Lake Erie.

    A. tunneled

    B. conquered

    C. erected

    D. hydrated

ANSWER EXPLANATIONS

READING LITERATURE

RL.1.1:
Supporting Statements

1. Part A - **C.** The end of the third paragraph says that the earth shook and trembled. There was an earthquake which forced the conductor to drive slower than usual. Answer choice A ".. he was late because the rails were 'made out of unsafe materials' may appear correct because the passage also mentions that the train driver was going slowly because he thought the "the rails might spread apart and an accident happen to his passengers", but answer choice A makes a statement of fact that the rails were made of unsafe materials, but the evidence in the passage does not support this.

Part B - **D.** This answer choice describes that the train was late because of an earthquake. A and B are incorrect as they only describe how the train moves, not why it is late. Part C only notes when the train was supposed to arrive.

2. **B.**   The little girl, Dorothy Gale, is going to Hugson's Ranch. She asks the little boy if he is going to take her there (paragraph 8). D may seem correct, but Hugson's Ranch is part of Hugson's Siding. One is the the town, whereas the other one is a specific location in the town.

3. **A.** The little girl does not at first see anyone inside the buggy. Finally, she notes the little boy laying asleep. This indicates that he has been waiting a long time (paragraph 5). She does have a difficult time spotting him, but this isn't because he isn't there. Instead, it is because he is asleep.

6. Part A - **B.** The girl shows the boy that his question does not make sense. She explains that she could not be with the boy if the train had not arrived.

Part B - **D.** This answer choice quotes the part of the text where the girl tells the boy that she could not be talking to him if the train had not arrived. Answer choice C is incorrect as it is another question and not a response. Answer choice A is incorrect as this answer choice relates to the boy's response later on in the passage, not the girl's response to his question of whether the train had arrived or not.

5. Part A - **C.** Paragraph 13 explains that Dorothy Gale felt the bird cage was the best way to transport her cat, Eureka.

Part B - **B.** Paragraph 13 explains that she is using the bird cage to carry her cat. She does not have

a bird with her, making C incorrect. A is incorrect because even though she sets the bird cage down, this does not clarify why she has it with her.

6. **C.**   In paragraph 5, the narrator discusses the girl's observations about the horse, the harness, and the buggy. Evidence supports that the horse is frail, the harness is in poor condition, but the buggy is almost new.

7. **Answers will vary.** [Example answer: She thinks that the boy is messy.   She is staring at him with serious eyes, noting the state of his uncombed hair.]

8. **Answers will vary.** [Example answer: Eureka is the girl's cat. Near the end of the passage, she indicates that she found the cat and named her Eureka, since the name means "I have found it" (paragraph 16).]

9.   **Answers will vary.** [Example answer: Dorothy is an observant girl.   As an observant girl, she noticed the condition of the boy's hair and the color of his eyes when, as the passage states, she "looked gravely at his tousled hair and blinking gray eyes."   She also noticed that the horse was very thin. Paragraph 5 states: "It was a big horse, tall and bony, with long legs and large knees and feet."   Her point of view of the buggy, as described in paragraph 5, also shows that she pays attention to details: "The buggy seemed almost new, for it had a shiny top and side curtains."]

RL.5.2:
Determine Theme & Summarize Text

1. Part A - **B.** Part B - **C.** Though Daedalus gives Icarus the warning about flying to high to the sun or the wax on his wings will melt, Icarus ignores his father's warning, which was intended to keep him safe.

2. **B.** Daedalus is put in prison early in the story. He's broken-hearted at the end of the story because Icarus disobeyed his warning. He faces the laws of nature as he learns how to fly and when he flies away with his wings. The power of the gods is absent from the story.

3. **C.** Though all the other summaries include some of the important details of the story, C highlights all the core events of the story.

4. **A.** The king's favor, described as "veer[ing] with the wind," is so easily swayed that he uses his power to imprison Daedalus even though he doesn't deserve it.

5. Part A - **D.** Part B - **C.** The boy doesn't work hard at the time everyone else is. Everyone else knows that it's the season to plant, but the boy doesn't. The "old man of the season," who represents time in the story, says that the "season has gone, and no man can bring it back," which implies that the boy has wasted time and can't get it back.

6. **Answers will vary.** [Example answer: Both stories highlight the need for young people to listen to the wisdom of those older than them. In Passage 1, Daedalus builds wings for his son to fly away with him. "Remember," he said, "never to fly very low or very high, for the fogs about the earth would weigh you down, but the blaze of the sun will surely melt your feathers apart if you go too near." Icarus doesn't heed his father's warning, however, and ends up dying as a result. In Passage 2, the boy neglects to work as hard as everyone else when the time is right. When he puts off the hard work until the season is over, he's confronted by a personification of the season, who says to him, "You should have ploughed when others did. The season has gone, and no man can bring it back." The boy foolishly chose not to plow when it was the season to do so, and he suffered the consequences of his choice.]

7. **B.** The boy's laziness brings about every other conflict that he faces in the story.

8. **Answers will vary.** [An example summary: A lazy boy neglected to plant his field when the time was right, and when he finally did begin to plant his field, he discovered it was too late. Even though he tried his best when he finally went to work, he found he could not make up for his wasted time.]

RL.5.3:
Compare and contrast two or more characters, settings, or events

1. Part A - **A.** The tin soldier was the first toy to speak up and suggest breaking the mistress' rules. It was not Raggedy Ann because she did not mention anything about moving until the tin man had already suggested it in paragraph 5. Part B - A. In paragraph 5, the tin soldier says, "Now let's have a good time." He also says, "Let's all go in search of something to eat."

2. Part A - **C** In paragraph 10, the other dolls clap to show their agreement with the Indian Doll. Part B - B In paragraph 10, the text states: "At this all the other dolls clapped their hands together and shouted, "Hurrah! Raggedy Ann will be our

leader." In Option A, only one doll expresses her approval. Although Option A and Option C indirectly relate to Raggedy Ann's leadership, neither is the best answer to specifically support the correct answer to Part A. Option D is not relevant in this case.

3. **B.** The dolls are determined. They encounter different problems, but they work together to find a solution. If they were not determined, they would not have been able to plan their route to the pantry, pick a leader, or help that leader when she realized she was injured. They also tried different ways to unlock the pantry and get inside. Yes, the dolls were hungry, but this does not directly relate to their ability to get inside the pantry. The dolls appear to have been disobedient, but this does not directly relate to using their abilities to get inside the pantry. There is no mention of the dolls becoming panicked. They worked together and overcame problems to get to the goodies.

4. **D.** This detail from the passage shows that all the dolls recognize Raggedy Ann's strong thinking skills. When they saw her sitting down, they did not think she had given up or was tired. Instead, they thought she was thinking things through. Option A is incorrect, since this simply refers to her getting her head repaired.

5. Part A - **D.** The Mole lives underground. The text discusses how he has to climb with his little paws to get up atop the earth. Part B - **D.** He came into the sunlight after he had climbed upward. This shows that he lives underground, otherwise he would not be climbing. All the other options are places he traveled to in the text.

6. Part A- **D.** The passage tells about spring arriving and is specific in sharing things about the leaves budding, the birds chirping, and even directly says that "Spring was moving in". Part B-**1st and 3rd choice**. Both the quotations indicate that spring is arriving. While spring is not directly referenced in Option C, the reference to flowers budding and birds building nests indicates the arrival of spring. The statement about the holiday does not directly relate to the events in the story. The other two statements are unrelated to spring.

7. **Answers will vary.** [Example answer: The Mole's attitude becomes more relaxed as he moves through the different places in the story. In the beginning, he is at his home underground and feels panicked. He is cleaning and not really enjoying himself. When he begins traveling, he is comparing his travels to cleaning, noting that

he would rather be moving around than cleaning/whitewashing. He is rushed and wants to keep moving until he arrives at the river. One he gets to the river, he is more relaxed and lingers. He is willing to pause and listen to the river.]

8. **B.** Option B best captures what the excerpt is describing and what the reader can infer from this description. Option C is incorrect as the description does not indicate anything about Mole being lazy. Option A and D are incorrect, as the references are misunderstandings about the metaphors and similes about the river (and Mole's relationship to it) that are mentioned in the excerpt.

RL.5.4:
Determine Word Meaning in Text

1. **C.** Based upon the context clues of Ashton fellow classmates whispering and laughing about him, we know that ridicule means teasing.

2. **D.** The context clues in the mom's dialogue indicate that she's worried about the effect Ashton's constant game-playing is having on him.

3. **A.** Although conjure is word referring to magic, the author of the passage is using it figuratively to communicate the idea of Ashton making a smile appear on his face.

4. **B.** The context of the story demonstrates that Ashton is unable to concentrate because of his video games.

5. **A.** Based on Mrs. Burhardt's dialogue to Ashton, she clearly thinks he has too much potential to not turn in his homework, which she refers to as his capability.

6. **B.** We know from the story that Ashton isn't literally piloting a ship. The author is comparing Ashton's life and his irresponsibility to a ship that is sinking.

7. **D.** Bright is being used as a synonym for good, not as a description of something shining.

8. **B.** This quote contains a comparison between Mrs. Burhardt and a witch.

RL.5.5:
Explain how a series of chapters, scenes, or stanzas fits together to provide the overall structure of a particular story, drama, or poem.

1. Part A - **A.** The first paragraph describes the setting. Readers gain an awareness of where the characters are as well as the activities that are currently occurring. There are no details about what happened in the past nor does this paragraph compare Maurya to the other characters. There is also no preview of future events, only what is currently happening. Part B - **D.** Paragraph 9 adds additional information about the setting, including that there is a turf-loft in the house. The paragraph also references waves and the tide, indicating that the cottage is close to the sea, another element of the setting. The other paragraphs are simply dialogue or describing an action being completed by the characters. There is no additional information about the setting in these other answer options.

2. **A.** The characters are most likely celebrating a birthday. They would not be buying/hiding gifts or baking a cake to mourn a loss. These activities would also not necessarily be associated with preparing to move. While the cake and gift could be associated with welcoming new neighbors, the girls are hiding the gift from Maurya in the turf-loft, so it would not make sense for the reason to be welcoming a new neighbor.

3. **C.** Towards the end of the play, the brother notes the need to board the boat because there will not be another one for several days. The passage mentions a boat, but only in the context of the brother needing to catch a boat, not a friend currently on a boat. The passage does not mention looking for seashells. While the weather might be bad, there are no details to support Cathleen's need to prepare the house for a storm.

4. **B.** The list of characters explains who the characters are and how they are related. It indicates who is the son, daughter, etc. It also gives an indication of who is oldest and youngest in the family. There are no other details provided in the character box, making the other options incorrect.

5. **A.** The words inside parentheses indicate that the character included in that paragraph are completing an activity. For example, in paragraph two the words inside parentheses (in a low voice) are giving Nora directions on how she should speak. In paragraph 5, the words in parentheses (spinning the wheel rapidly) indicate how Cathleen should spin the wheel while she speaks.

6. **B.** The person viewing the jellyfish sees it, and then s/he no longer sees it. There are no details about the jellyfish being trapped in a net. While it does open/close/float away, there are no details

to support that the jellyfish attacks. The jellyfish's color is mentioned, but there are no details about the color changing.

7. **A.** "The blue surrounding it grows cloudy…" indicates that the jellyfish is no longer visible. This indicates that the visibility of the water is changing, and thus the jellyfish is disappearing from view as it floats away. This is why the jellyfish goes from being 'visible' to 'invisible'.

8. **Answers may vary.** [Example answer: The facts learned about the jellyfish include that the jellyfish opens and closes when it moves. Another fact is that it is orange in color, which is inferred from the line stating it is an "amber-colored amethyst".]

RL.5.6:
Describe How Point of View Influences Events

1. **A.** The narrator is telling Emily's story, but Emily herself is not the narrator.

2. Part A - **C.** Part B - **C.** The context of the entire story communicates that Emily is afraid of the rain, but the way she says "thunder" when asked by her mom what is wrong clearly shows she's afraid.

3. Answers will vary, but the student will likely mention the fact that the mom isn't afraid of the rain. The student may comment on how the mom feels about Emily's fear of the rain with either compassion or frustration at being woke up over it.

4. **Answers will vary.** [Example answer: The narrator implies that Emily is a young child. It mentions that the thunder caused her to jump "out of bed and run to her parent's room," which indicates that she lives with her parents. She refer to her mother as "Mommy," a term usually used by small children. Finally, she climbs into bed with her parents and sleeps between them. All of this evidence indicates that Emily is a little girl.]

5. **B.** The story is told in first-person, using first-person pronouns, from the perspective of the girl telling her own story.

6. Part A - **B.** Part B - **D.** The narrator recalls playing in the rain when she was younger and then decides, as she's watching the rain, that it's been too long since she's played in the rain, clearly indicating that she loves the rain.

7. **Answers will vary.** [Example answer: Both passages describe a time when there was a storm and/or rain. In Passage 1, the feeling the reader gets about the rain/storm is that it is something to be afraid of. In Passage 2, however, the rain/storm is presented as something to be enjoyed and that might even create a welcoming environment in which to play and have fun. Passage 1 focuses on the loud scary sounds of thunder during rain, while Passage 2 focuses on the light tapping of rain on a window and the low rumble of thunder.]

8. Answers will vary, but given that Emily is afraid of the rain/storm, it's likely that she wouldn't look outside with fond memories about playing in the rain. She'd likely describe it in terms that are more destructive and something to hide from, rather as a way to have fun.

RL.5.7:
Analyze How Images Contribute to Text

1. **B.** The first two paragraphs describe a visit by the Town Mouse to the Country Mouse's home. They eat and then enjoy a comfortable night of sleep. The tone isn't suspenseful, humorous, or gloomy, but lighthearted.

2. **A.** The two mice are about to enjoy a large luxurious meal when a cat, the mice's natural predator shows up, causing them to run and hide. When they try to return, people and a dog keep them from feeling confident enough to get some food. They're optimistic at the beginning of paragraph 3, but they become frightened with the cat, dog, and people.

3. **B.** Though the text in Passage 1 doesn't describe a chase by the cat, the image helps the reader to see the encounter with the cat more intensely. There's no necessary contrast, since a chase could have happened in the story and was only hinted at. The story doesn't end tragically. The encounter doesn't feel playful.

4. **Answers will vary.** [Example answer: The main difference the author of Passage 1 describes is the difference between the food in the country and the town. The Country Mouse serves his friend, the Town Mouse, "wheat stalks, roots, and acorns, with a dash of cold water to drink." The Town Mouse isn't used to this kind of food and eats "the simple food only to be polite." The Town Mouse lives in a mansion and leads the Country Mouse to the dining room, where they find "the leavings of a very fine banquet. There

were sweetmeats and jellies, pastries, delicious cheeses, indeed, the most tempting foods that a Mouse can imagine." There is a clear contrast between the simplicity of living in the country and the luxury of living in the town.]

5. **B.** Passage 2, when read from beginning to end, is clearly meant to teach a lesson about being careful of underestimating the abilities of others. Students could be tempted to pick A because the story mentions the Hare being amused, and there is a sense of irony to the story, but it's more cautionary than humored. It gives the feel neither of dread nor peace.

6. **Answers will vary.** [Example answer: The image shows the Tortoise ahead of the Hare and the Hare trying to catch up. This is described near the end of paragraph 6. The Hare seems to have an almost frantic look on his face, while the Tortoise gives a slight smile. It seems clear that this image belongs at the end of the story when the Hare can't catch up to the Tortoise and loses the race.]

7. **C.** The Tortoise wears a smile that is almost smug or amused as he moves past the sleeping Hare. A is true, but this is not an enhancement of the story - just a detail that is illustrated.

8. **B.** It's indisputable that the Hare is faster than the Tortoise, so the story doesn't communicate the idea that everyone has the same ability levels.

RL.5.9:
Compare & Contrast Stories in Same Genre

1. **D.** While both passages talk about winning and losing, Passage 1 ends with a loss, and Passage 2 doesn't reveal if the team won.

2. Part A - **C.** Part B - **B.** Jared is driven to win more than anything because he wants to make his dad happy.

3. Part A - **B.** Part B - **D.** Because of the advice of his dad, Trey has learned to just enjoy playing the game, regardless of the outcome of the game.

4. **B.** It's clear from the context of both passages that Jared knows that losing the game will mean disappointment from his father, but Trey's father supports him whether he wins or loses.

5. **Answers will vary.** [Example answer: The boys' relationships with their fathers is clearly what most influences how they play the game. Jared's dad is not at all supportive if Jared doesn't

play well, so Jared is focused solely on winning; he can't enjoy the game and wants to quit when the game does not go his team's way. Trey's father is supportive and encourages him that enjoying the game is more important than anything. Because of this, Trey loves playing whether he wins or loses.]

6. **B.** Since the story is about focusing on the process of the game rather than the outcome of the game, the author chose to not include the game's result since it was irrelevant to the purpose of the story.

7. **Answers will vary.** [Example answer: Because Trey's father is supportive and is only interested in his son having fun playing baseball, it's likely that Jared wouldn't have felt the pressure to tie up the game for his team. Instead, he would have given his best and enjoyed playing and wouldn't have been devastated if he lost because he would know his father still supported him.]

8. **D.** Both boys approach baseball because of the way their fathers treat them in relation to the game.

READING INFORMATION
RI.5.1:
Quote Accurately and Draw Inferences from a Text

1. Part A - **D.** Part B - **B.** After his death, Mansa Musa's descendants lost most of his fortune. This is supported by the quote explaining that Musa's descendants couldn't maintain his fortune.

2. **Answers will vary.** Students may select quotes such as, "Mansa Musa oversaw the construction of several schools, including the University of Timbuktu…Many scholars believe that the University of Timbuktu was the world's first university," and, "Musa tried to rectify the gold market by borrowing all the gold he could from Cairo's money-lenders, at high interest. This is the only time in recorded history that one man directly controlled the price of gold in the Mediterranean."

3. **Answers will vary.** [Example answer: Mansa Musa expanded the empire, constructed many important buildings, and increased education, to name a few of his accomplishments. The text states that, "Mansa Musa oversaw the construction

of several schools," and that Musa "expanded the borders of the Mali Empire, advanced education, and constructed many important buildings." It also says that his reign "brought culture, architecture, trade, wealth, and education to the Mali Empire."]

4. Part A - **A.** Part B - **B.** The text explains that Musa's journeys were beneficial for two reason: they brought recognition to the Mali Empire and allowed Musa to bring important people, including architects and scholars, back to Mali. Although answer choice B does not provide evidence for this entire statement, it does give the best evidence of the provided choices. It demonstrates that Mansa Musa's trips allowed him to recruit important people to return to Mali.

5. Alexander's father cried tears of joy because he felt that Alexander's ability to ride Bucephalus showed he would be a good, strong king. No one else could ride Bucephalus, "not even the greatest men in the kingdom." This probably made Alexander's father believe that Alexander would grow up to be a great and powerful man, which meant the "kingdom would continue to prosper after his death."

6. Part A - **C.** Part B - **C.** Readers can infer that leaders wanted to imitate Alexander because he was a brilliant military leader. He wasn't admired and respected by his subjects, and the article doesn't provide evidence that he was generous or extremely wealthy. The quotation explaining that Alexander had conquered most of the known world is the best evidence to support this answer.

7. **Answers will vary.** Students may select quotes such as, "Although he was very successful, Alexander was not a popular or beloved king," or, "He had a terrible temper, drank too much wine, and was ruthless to anyone who dared oppose him—even his friends." This quote shows even Alexander's own subjects and friends could have had a motive to murder him. He had many enemies from other nations too, as demonstrated by quotes like, "To show that he would not be a weak king, Alexander swiftly put down these rebellions and executed their leaders."

8. **Answers will vary.** Students may select quotes such as, "Although Alexander the Great only lived to the age of 32, he is considered one of history's most powerful leaders and most dominant military minds," or, "By the age of only 26, Alexander had conquered the Persian Empire."

RI.5.2:
Determine Main Idea and Summarize Text

1. **C.** The other answer choices are too specific, not giving an overall idea of what the article is about. The main focus of the article is on explaining the condition of synesthesia.

2. Sentences **2** and **5** are the best pieces of information to include in a summary of the text. Both contribute to explaining what synesthesia is, while the other quotes provide specific details that would not need to be included in a summary.

3. **Answers will vary.** [Example answer: Since the brain reacts in a few different ways, depending on which senses are being blended, scientists aren't sure how synesthesia occurs or what causes it. The article states that scientists will likely learn more as advances are made in brain imaging technology and research.]

4. **B.** This answer choice describes the way that some synesthetes view synesthesia. The use of the phrase, "On the other hand," shows that some feel differently, indicating mixed feelings about the condition.

5. **Answers will vary.** [Example answer: The main idea of Passage A is that the power of words have influenced the history of our country, from the American Revolution to the formation of our government. The article explains that powerful quotes like, "Give me liberty or give me deaths!" helped convince more American colonists to support the fight for independence. It also mentions that the powerful words in the Declaration of Independence and the Articles of Confederation created the United States.]

6. Part A - **C.** Part B - **C.** The Articles of

Confederation were rewritten because they initially created a weak government that couldn't maintain order. This was best illustrated by Shays' Rebellion. After the rebellion, Alexander Hamilton called a convention to write stronger laws that would establish more order in the new nation. Answer choice C does the best job of explaining this. It specifically mentions both the Constitution and the Articles of Confederation, and it specifies that the Constitution achieved the goal of creating a stronger government. This implies that the Articles, by contrast, created a weak government.

7. **B.** This answer choice best generalizes the focus of this passage. The others provide overly specific details. Additionally, both the introduction and conclusion mention the power of words, emphasizing that it's the main idea of the passage.

8. Part A - **A.** Part B - **D.** The Constitution created stronger laws than the Articles of Confederation in an effort to maintain order and calm the chaos. This is best demonstrated by answer choice D. It states that the Constitution established a perfect balance between freedom and order. The Articles of Confederation already established freedom, so order was what they obviously lacked. The quote also states that "the chaos died down," showing that these stronger laws helped maintain order.

RI.5.3:
Explain Relationships Between Individuals, Events, and Ideas

1. **B.** The government wanted to make construction of the transcontinental railroad faster, so they passed the Pacific Railroad Act declaring that both Central Pacific Railroad Company and the Union Pacific Railroad would work on its construction.

2. Students should select 1, 3, 4, and 7. Construction was slowed down by the mountains, bad weather, attacks from Native Americans, and the Civil War. 5 and 6 weren't mentioned at all in the article, and competition between the two railroads (2) only sped up construction.

3. Part A - **A.** Part B - **D.** Each company would earn money and land from the government for every mile of railroad constructed, so each company was rushing to complete more of the railroad in order to get more money and more land. Efforts were made to speed up the process by using nitroglycerin to get through the Sierra Nevada, which resulted in deaths. Workers also built weak tracks in their hurry, and these had to be rebuilt later.

4. **Answers will vary.** [Example answer: The Central Pacific Railroad Company was faced with the obstacle of the Sierra Nevada Mountains. This meant that workers had to blast through granite, sometimes making only a two- or three-inch dent in the mountain by the end of the day's work.]

5. **Answers will vary.** [Example answer: Railroad workers from the Central Pacific Railroad Company started to use nitroglycerin to blast through the Sierra Nevada Mountains more quickly. This did greatly speed up the process, but some railroad workers died from nitroglycerin explosions.]

6. **C.** President Ulysses Grant asked the two companies to decide where the railroads would meet, and they selected Promontory Summit in Utah.

7. **Answers will vary.** [Example answer: The transcontinental railroad made travel faster and cheaper in the United States. It allowed people, ideas, and goods to travel more freely. People were able to conduct business cross-country, and even more settlers journeyed west.]

8. **Answers will vary.** [Example answer: The transcontinental railroad negatively impacted by the United States by destroying many natural resources. It also had a negative impact on the Native American way of life, as the railroad was built through tribal lands.]

RI.5.4:
Determine Academic and Domain-Specific Word Meaning in Text

1. **C.** This is the most accurate definition because it contains key information found in the text.

For each biome, the text mentions plants, animals, and climate. The other definitions are vague or incomplete.

2. **B.** Plants can't grow when the soil is frozen. They may also be unable to spread or exist, but these options sound awkward when placed in the sentence, making "grow" a better definition. Option A is incorrect because the soil would have no effect on the amount of sunlight the plants can receive.

3. **B.** Options B-D are plants, but the sentence specifies that the plant is "low," meaning it can't be a "giant" conifer known for its "great height." The plant is also compared to moss, which makes it more likely to be something that forms a growth, rather than a shrub or clump of shrubs.

4. **D.** "Occupy" is the only word that makes sense in this context. The animals don't captivate or endanger their biomes, and "habitually" is an adverb. A verb is needed in this sentence.

5. **C.** The animals rarely depart from their home. Originate and arrive don't make sense in this context, and "flee" means to run from something. This sounds too dramatic for this context, and there's nothing in the sentence that would suggest fleeing rather than departing.

6. **B.** The use of the word "but" indicates that "plethora" must contrast with "few." For this reason, "large amount" is the most logical answer.

7. **C.** The desert is extremely dry. 10 inches of rain weekly or daily does not fit this description. 10 inches of rain ever is too extreme. Thus, the best answer is "yearly."

8. **Answers will vary.** [Example answer: A nocturnal animal is most active at night. The sentence mentions that many desert animals are nocturnal "to avoid daytime heat." This suggests that the desert animals stay hidden during the day and come out at night.]

RI.5.5:
Compare & Contrast Structure of Events, Ideas or Information in Texts

1. Part A - **D.** Part B - **See explanation**. The text begins by describing a problem, which is people living in tornado alley and the potential for destruction and death. The text describes tornados as "one of the most violent types of severe weather." It also mentions that they "can cause significant property damage and even loss of life." After presenting the problem, the text offers a solution, storm shelters. The text says, "Storm shelters or safe rooms can give families living in tornado alley the protection of a room with walls that can withstand the dangerous high winds of the strongest tornadoes."

2. **B.** A and C don't fit because there's no other mention of hurricanes in the text. C changes the point-of-view from third person to first person.

3. **C.** The reader needs to understand why interior rooms aren't as safe as storm shelters.

4. **A.** Because the text is structured as problem and solution, the author writes to offer a solution to the danger of tornadoes in tornado alley.

5. Part A - **A.** Part B - **See explanation.** The text is structured by a comparison and contrast of tornadoes and hurricanes. The text demonstrates similarity of tornadoes and hurricanes when it says, "They're both caused by an instability in atmospheric conditions and both produce extreme winds, which can cause destruction." The difference is described when the text says, "Tornados form as a rotating column of air on land. Hurricanes, however, are cyclones that only form on water."

6. **B.** The author is showing how tornados and hurricanes are similar.

7. **Answers will vary.** [Example answer: Both texts describe tornadoes and their destructive nature. Passage 1 focuses on a solution to the threat of tornadoes. Passage 2, however, compares and contrasts tornadoes with hurricanes.]

8. **C.** Both texts mention the destructive winds caused by tornadoes.

RI.5.6:
Analyze & Compare/Contrast Multiple Accounts of Same Topic

1. **C.** The author gives arguments for why he believes that pit bulls are a dangerous type of dog for families to own.

2. **B.** The way the author talks about pit bulls indicates that he does not trust them to be safe companion.

3. **D.** The author clearly communicates an aversion to pit bulls from the perspective of an outside observer.

4. **D.** The author highlights the need for people to change their negative opinion of pit bells.

5. **D.** The author argues that pit bull attacks have been overly exaggerated.

6. **B.** Both authors acknowledge the tendencies of pit bulls to be aggressive.

7. **A.** The author of passage one argues that pit bull attacks are more prevalent than attacks by other dogs, so he would agree that pit bulls are more aggressive than other dogs.

8. **Answers will vary.** [Example answer: The author of Passage 1 seems to have a dislike for pit bulls. He begins by stating that pit bulls "are some of the most dangerous dogs in the world." After discussing pit bull attacks, the author ends by arguing that "people in general aren't responsible enough to own pit bulls." This contrasts with the author of Passage 2, who clearly loves pit bulls, especially her own. She agrees with the author of Passage 1 that pit bulls can be aggressive and that "there have been reports of them attacking people, but these attacks aren't as prevalent as most people are led to believe." Each author writes from their personal feelings about pit bulls.]

RI.5.8:
Explain How Authors Use Evidence to Support Points of View

1. Part A - **C.** Part B - **D.** Though the author makes each of the points listed, the primary idea that ties it all together is that Dr. Seuss inspired many children to become readers with his books.

2. **A.** While B and D both mention the idea of children reading more, A explicitly mentions both entertainment and education as motivations behind writing The Cat and the Hat.

3. **D.** The other answers are assertions of fact. D is an assertion of the author's opinion that Seuss is most well-known for The Cat in the Hat, which is debatable, making it opinion rather than fact.

4. **B.** It was Seuss's writing style that made his books appeal to children in a way that others did not.

5. Part A - **D.** Part B - **B.** Before becoming an author, Geisel was an illustrator and cartoonist, and he did really well at it. The quote in B alludes to the idea that Geisel could have continued in the career he was in, but he decided to write for children instead.

6. **Answers will vary.** [Example answer: The author mentions that Dr. Seuss didn't have any children of his own when he began writing for children and that he began writing for children during the same time that he found out his wife couldn't have children. Evidence from the text a student might provide comes from paragraph 6, "It is interesting to note that Dr. Seuss wrote his first children's book the same year that he found out his wife, Helen, could not have children. Perhaps Dr. Seuss wrote for children to help fill a void in his own life."]

7. **Answers will vary.** [Example answer: "Dr. Seuss became one of the most well-known writers of children's books, creating stories that were fun and had a lyrical quality to them." "As demonstrated in many of the other stories written by Dr. Seuss, Seuss's style of telling stories in whimsical rhymes with fun

illustrations made reading enjoyable again for many children."]

8. **Answers will vary.** The student may respond by pointing out that the author is demonstrating that Dr. Seuss is still relevant even several decades after he began publishing his books. It's likely that the student will have experienced reading a Dr. Seuss book or seeing a film adaptation of one, and so s/he will be able to provide personal examples.

RI.5.9:
Integrate & Explain Information from Several Texts

1. **B.** A is inaccurate. Option C puts the focus on segregation instead of on Dr. King. Option D focuses on a supporting detail rather than the main idea. Option B captures the core of what the passage is about.

2. Part A - **D.** Part B - **D.** Dr. King urged people to protest without violence, so he wasn't motivated by it.

3. **C.** B and D focus on supporting details of the passage. Option C best captures the core of what the passage is about. Option A only focuses on one aspect of King in the passage.

4. **D.** Both passages characterize Dr. King as someone who cares about the rights of all people, which made him willing to defend those rights. Option A is incorrect because he was against violence. Option B is incorrect because neither passage comments upon his speaking ability. Option C is incorrect because he isn't characterized as angry, and he never tried to control anyone.

5. **A.** Paragraph 4 makes this clear when it mentions that Dr. King was arrested for refusing to leave a whites-only department store lunch counter.

6. **D.** Passage 1 mentions his birth date, and Passage 2 mentions the date of his death. The math reveals that he was 39 when he died.

7. **A.** Both quotes mention King's inspiration in the Bible's teaching that God created all people equal.

8. **Answers will vary.** [Example answer: Passage 2 mentions specific examples of discrimination with white-only bus seats and water fountains. It mentions the Civil Rights Movement of the 1950s and 1960s. It mentions why Dr. King was arrested and how he was freed. Finally, it mentions when and how Dr. King died.]

LANGUAGE

L.1.1:
Have Command of Grammar & Usage

L.5.1A
Understand Conjunctions, Prepositions, and Interjections

1. **A.** The interjection in this sentence is the word "Stop!" The other answer choices are incorrect.

2. **C.** The preposition in this sentence is the word "with." The other answer choices are incorrect.

3. **B.** The best preposition in the context of this sentence is the word "across," showing that the firetruck moved on the floor.

4. Jonathan's uncle has been looking for a job, <u>but</u> he is still able to pay his bills from his savings account.

L.5.1B:
Form and Use Perfect Verb Tenses

1. **C.** The phrase "will have finished" is an example of future perfect tense.

2. **B.** The correct form of the verb to complete this sentence is "should have." The other answer choices are incorrect.

3. **B.** Answer choice B is the correct way to write the sentence is present perfect verb tense. The other answer choices are incorrect.

ANSWER EXPLANATIONS

4.

Verb Tense	Sentence
Perfect	I had run for 20 minutes when my brother called me back home.
present perfect	I have run in several marathons.
past perfect	I will have run 8 miles by the end of the week.

L.5.1C:
Use Verb Tense to Convey Time, Sequences, States, and Conditions

1. **A.** This sentence correctly uses the verb "win" in past tense. The other answer choices are incorrect.

2. **B.** This revised sentence correctly uses the verb "walk" in future tense. The other answer choices are incorrect.

3. **D.** Answer choice D is the only sentence correctly written in present tense.

4. **Answers will vary.** [Example answer: Yesterday at school we learned about fractions. Today we are taking a test on fractions, and we are also getting an extra long recess. Tomorrow it will be the weekend, and I hope to play basketball with my cousins.]

L.5.1D:
Understand Shifts in Verb Tense

1. **C.** This answer choice correctly uses the past tense with no shift.

2. Part A - **D.** This answer choice correctly uses past tense.

Part B - **A.** The reader understands the need for verbs to be written in past tense because of the introductory phrase, "Last week."

3. **B.** The correct use of the verb "left" in this sentence is "had left," which is past perfect tense.

4. **Answers will vary.** [Example answer: Once upon a time, there was a girl who loved to spend summers at swim camp. There, she did many of her favorite things. She played water polo. She went swimming. She got to hang out with some of her best friends. She made many friendships at swim camp and couldn't wait to go back!]

L.5.1E:
Use Correlative Conjunctions

1. **C.** The correct correlative conjunctions for this sentence are no sooner/ than, showing the relationship of time.

2. **A.** The correct correlative conjunctions for this sentence are not only/ but also, showing a comparison relationship.

3.

Correlative Conjunctions	Sentence
either, or	Either I am a mistaken, or there are less students in my class than last year.
neither, nor	Neither the dog nor the cat could be found in the house.

4. **Answers will vary.** [Example answer: Neither Dayton nor Juliana like carrots.]

L.5.2:
Know Capitalization, Punctuation, & Spelling

L.5.2A:
Use Punctuation to Separate Items

1. **A.** Commas belong after each item in the series. Therefore, A is the correct answer.

2.

Series	Series with Punctuation
wake up brush my teeth eat breakfast and catch the bus	wake up, brush my teeth, eat breakfast, and catch the bus
Jessica Lori Pam and Jasmine	Jessica, Lori, Pam, and Jasmine
chicken green beans potatoes and sweet tea	chicken, green beans, potatoes, and sweet tea

3. **B.** A comma is missing after the word Skittles, as the second to last item in the series.

4. Our basketball uniform consists of a shirt, shorts, socks, and a sweatband.

L.5.2B:
Use Commas to Separate Introductions

1. **A.** The comma separates the introductory phrase "At the movies" from the independent clause "I will buy popcorn." The other answer choices are incorrect.

2. **C.** A comma belongs after the word "start." This separates the introductory phrase "When it is time for school to start," from the independent clause "the bell will ring."

3. **C.** This sentence correctly places a comma after the introductory phrase "While eating dinner." The other answer choices are incorrect.

4. **Answers will vary.** [Example answer: In summary, I believe that eagles are the most majestic bird.]

L.5.2C:
Use Commas for Tag Questions and Indirect Address

1. **C.** This answer choice is correct because a comma sets off the word "yes."

2. **B.** This answer choice is correct because a comma sets off the word "please."

3. [Example answer: They won't cheat, will they?]

4. **B.** The correct tag question for this statement is "didn't you?" The other answer choices are incorrect.

L.5.2D:
Use Correct Grammar to Indicate Titles of Works

1. **B.** This answer choice is correct because the book title is underlined.

2. **A.** This answer choice is correct because the article title is in quotation marks.

3. **A.** This answer choice is correct because the short story title is italicized.

4. [Example answer: When I was younger, my favorite book was Corduroy, but now that I'm older, I prefer the book Bridge to Terabithia.]

L.5.2E:
Spell Correctly

1. **B.** This question asks to identify the incorrect word spelling. In answer choice B the word "presentation" is spelled incorrectly.

2. **D.** This answer choice is correct because it correctly uses the homophone "sent." The other homophones are used incorrectly. A homophone is one of two or more words pronounced alike but different in meaning or derivation or spelling.

3. **B.** The correct answer choice and spelling is "cell." The other homophones and spellings are incorrect.

4. **Answers will vary.** [Example answer: Before we headed outside to the creek, my dad and I had to go up to our attic to find our water shoes. The boards in the attic creaked as we looked through old boxes.]

L.5.3:
Understand & Use appropriate Language Conventions
L.5.3A:
Expand, Combine, and Reduce Sentences

1. **B.** This revision makes the sentence more effective by describing how Bradley waited and giving a specific description of his lunch.

2. **Answers will vary.** [Example answer: Joe wanted to play hockey, but he couldn't skate very well.]

3. **A.** This revision is the best choice because it combines the ideas while including the most relevant details.

4. **D.** "So" is the best conjunction because it shows the that the mother let the children sleep on the floor due to their fear.

5. **Answers will vary.** [Example answer: The impatient man waited irritably for hours for his car to be repaired.]

L.5.3B:
Compare and Contrast Varieties of English

1. **D.** The variety of language that a group of people speak is called dialect. The other answers choices are incorrect.

2. **B.** This example of Southern dialect is best rewritten by answer choice B. The other answer choices do not accurately translate the sentence.

3. **C.** Mr. Pendanski uses formal register, contrasted by the informal nicknames of the boys.

4. **Answers will vary.** [Example answer: Good morning. I'd like to inquire what you are doing tonight. I'm considering joining some friends for dinner. Would you like to join me?]

5. **A.** Twain uses dialect to develop characters. The dialect shows that Jim is a commoner, perhaps less educated that Huck whose dialect is not very pronounced.

L.5.4:
Determine Meaning of Unknown Words When Reading

L.5.4A:
Use Context Clues

1. **C.** Given the context, the meaning that best fits the word "procession" is 'a group walking'. The other answer choices do not fit the context of the story.

2. Part A - **B.** The phrase "blue lips" implies that the family was cold.

Part B - **A.** This is supported by the detail that "children cuddled under one old quilt, trying to keep warm," which shows that they were cold.

3. **B.** "Huddled" means that the children were crowded on the bed. This is supported by the context clue that there were many of them in one bed.

4. **Answers will vary.** [Example answer: "Piling" means stacking. The context clue "one big plate" helps the reader understand that Meg is stacking the bread on a plate."]

L.5.4B:
Use Green and Latin Affixes and Roots

1. **B.** The root word port means "carry." Adding the prefix ex- changes the meaning to "carry away."

2.

Root	Meaning	My Word
photo	light	photograph
rupt	break or burst	rupture
script	to write	manuscript
dict	to say or tell	diction

3. **C.** The root "legal" is the correct answer. Legal means "allowed by law" and the prefix il- means "not." Therefore, the word illegal means "not allowed by law," and supports the idea that stealing is against the law.

4. [Example answer: The suffix -ian means one having a skill, which is explained in this sentence by identifying the skills of the person who performs magic and the person who fixes electronics.]

L.5.4C:
Use Reference Materials to Determine Meaning

1. **C.** The meaning of the word "civil" as it is used in context is courteous and polite. By adding the prefix un- the word "uncivil" means "rude."

2. **B.** The best synonym for "uncivil" is rude in the context of this passage. Other answers may be used as synonyms, but not in the context of this passage.

3. **Answers will vary.** [Example answer: The word "bewilder" means to cause to be confused. This makes sense in the context of this passage because Stevenson is confused by the newsboy acting both kind and rude.]

4. **C.** The best definition of the word "present" in this context is as a noun, meaning "a gift." The other answer choices do not fit the context of the passage.

L.5.5:
Understand Figurative Language and Word Relationships

L.5.5A:
Interpret Figurative Language

1. **A.** The phrase "piece of cake" means that something was easy. This is supported by context clues like "writing the paper was no problem."

2. **C.** The phrase "sea of people" indicates a crowd of a lot of people. Therefore, the answer choice "busy crowd" is the best answer.

3. Answers will vary. **[Example answer: the me**taphor is comparing the speaker's dad and a bear. They are alike because her dad wakes up grumpy like a bear.]

4. **Answers will vary.** [Example answer: The clouds in the sky were as fluffy as marshmallows.]

L.5.5B:
Recognize and Explain Idioms, Adages, and Proverbs

1. **B.** The phrase "raining cats and dogs" means that it's raining hard. The other answer choices are not accurate.

2. **C.** The correct word to fill in the blank is "book." The other answer choices are incorrect.

3. **C.** The idiom "died laughing" means that the person laughed abundantly. The phrase "father dressed up as a baby" helps the reader understand what the speaker is laughing about.

4. [Example answers: "Butterflies in her stomach" means that Jana is nervous. "Caught the eye" means that Jana and Sally looked at one another. "Break a leg" is an idiom that means "good luck" because in the theater it is considered bad luck to wish someone "good luck."]

L.5.5C:
Understand Word Relationships

1. **A.** The word "frequently" most nearly replaces the word "usually" as its synonym.

2. **B.** The homograph "match" is defined as "a contest in which people or teams compete" in the context of this sentence. Although the other definitions are accurate for the word "match," none fit in this context.

3. **D.** The word "loud" is not a synonym of "irate" in the context of this sentence. The other answer choices could all be synonyms.

4.

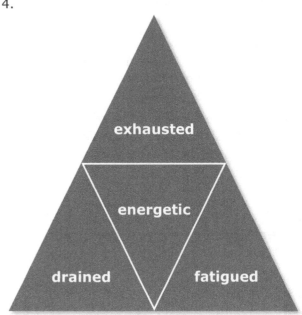

L.5.6:
Know & Use General Academic/ Domain-Specific Words

1. **D.** The word "grave" most nearly means "stern." The reader understand that Mamma is stern because her son can't stop wiggling.

2. **A.** The reader understand that the word "fidgety" means that he can't sit still, supported by that and other lines in the text.

3. **B.** The word that can most nearly replace "bade" is "told." No other answer choice makes sense to replace "bade."

4. **Answers will vary.** [Example answer: The poem says that Philip was in disgrace after he pulled all the dishes, etc. off the table.

Disgrace means shame, which the reader can tell by phrases like "Mamma did fret and frown" and "Papa made such a face."]

5. **A.** The word "resist" is best replaced by the word "survive." No other answer choice accurately conveys that hardy crops are able to stay alive in freezing conditions.

6. **C.** The word "sufficient" is best replaced by the word "adequate." No other answer choice accurately conveys that there is enough space in the classroom.

7. **C.** The word "however" shows a contrast between the supplies everyone was asked to bring and what participants actually brought.

8. **B.** The word "similarly" compares the cost of the shoes and the cost of the socks.

9. **D.** The word "although" most accurately fills in the blank, showing the relationship of being sick to taking the math test.

10. **A.** The word "tunneled" most accurately fills in the blank, showing that the canal was dug.

NY STATE STANDARDS ASSESSMENT

PRACTICE TESTS

NY STATE STANDARDS ASSESSMENT

ELA
Practice Test One

Session One

Directions: Read this passage. Then answer questions 1-7.

Passage 1: "President Obama's National Address to America's Schoolchildren" (Excerpt)
by Barack Obama

1   But at the end of the day, the circumstances of your life -- what you look like, where you come from, how much money you have, what you've got going on at home -- none of that is an excuse for neglecting your homework or having a bad attitude in school. That's no excuse for talking back to your teacher, or cutting class, or dropping out of school. There is no excuse for not trying.

2   Where you are right now doesn't have to determine where you'll end up. No one's written your destiny for you, because here in America, you write your own destiny. You make your own future.

3   That's what young people like you are doing every day, all across America.

4   Young people like Jazmin Perez, from Roma, Texas. Jazmin didn't speak English when she first started school. Neither of her parents had gone to college. But she worked hard, earned good grades, and got a scholarship to Brown University -- is now in graduate school, studying public health, on her way to becoming Dr. Jazmin Perez.

5   I'm thinking about Andoni Schultz, from Los Altos, California, who's fought brain cancer since he was three. He's had to endure all sorts of treatments and surgeries, one of which affected his memory, so it took him much longer -- hundreds of extra hours -- to do his schoolwork. But he never fell behind. He's headed to college this fall.

6   And then there's Shantell Steve, from my hometown of Chicago, Illinois. Even when bouncing from foster home to foster home in the toughest neighborhoods in the city, she managed to get a job at a local health care center, start a program to keep young people out of gangs, and she's on track to graduate high school with honors and go on to college.

7   And Jazmin, Andoni, and Shantell aren't any different from any of you. They face challenges in their lives just like you do...But they refused to give up. They chose to take responsibility for their lives, for their education, and set goals for themselves. And I expect all of you to do the same.

8   That's why today I'm calling on each of you to set your own goals for your education -- and do everything you can to meet them. Your goal can be something as simple as doing all your homework, paying attention in class, or spending some time each day reading a book. Maybe you'll decide to get involved in an extracurricular activity, or volunteer in your community. Maybe you'll decide to stand up for kids who are being teased or bullied because of who they are or how they look, because you believe, like I do, that all young people deserve a safe environment to

study and learn. Maybe you'll decide to take better care of yourself so you can be more ready to learn... But whatever you resolve to do, I want you to commit to it. I want you to really work at it.

9   I know that sometimes you get that sense from TV that you can be rich and successful without any hard work -- that your ticket to success is through rapping or basketball or being a reality TV star. Chances are you're not going to be any of those things.

10   The truth is, being successful is hard. You won't love every subject that you study. You won't click with every teacher that you have. Not every homework assignment will seem completely relevant to your life right at this minute. And you won't necessarily succeed at everything the first time you try.

11   That's okay. Some of the most successful people in the world are the ones who've had the most failures. J.K. Rowling's -- who wrote Harry Potter -- her first Harry Potter book was rejected 12 times before it was finally published. Michael Jordan was cut from his high school basketball team. He lost hundreds of games and missed thousands of shots during his career. But he once said, "I have failed over and over and over again in my life. And that's why I succeed."

12   These people succeeded because they understood that you can't let your failures define you -- you have to let your failures teach you. You have to let them show you what to do differently the next time. So if you get into trouble, that doesn't mean you're a troublemaker, it means you need to try harder to act right. If you get a bad grade, that doesn't mean you're stupid, it just means you need to spend more time studying.

13   No one's born being good at all things. You become good at things through hard work. You're not a varsity athlete the first time you play a new sport. You don't hit every note the first time you sing a song. You've got to practice. The same principle applies to your schoolwork. You might have to do a math problem a few times before you get it right. You might have to read something a few times before you understand it. You definitely have to do a few drafts of a paper before it's good enough to hand in.

14   Don't be afraid to ask questions. Don't be afraid to ask for help when you need it. I do that every day. Asking for help isn't a sign of weakness, it's a sign of strength because it shows you have the courage to admit when you don't know something, and that then allows you to learn something new. So find an adult that you trust -- a parent, a grandparent or teacher, a coach or a counselor -- and ask them to help you stay on track to meet your goals.

15   And even when you're struggling, even when you're discouraged, and you feel like other people have given up on you, don't ever give up on yourself, because when you give up on yourself, you give up on your country.

16   The story of America isn't about people who quit when things got tough. It's about people who kept going, who tried harder, who loved their country too much to do anything less than their best.

17 It's the story of students who sat where you sit 250 years ago, and went on to wage a revolution and they founded this nation. Young people. Students who sat where you sit 75 years ago who overcame a Depression and won a world war; who fought for civil rights and put a man on the moon. Students who sat where you sit 20 years ago who founded Google and Twitter and Facebook and changed the way we communicate with each other.

18 So today, I want to ask all of you, what's your contribution going to be? What problems are you going to solve? What discoveries will you make? What will a President who comes here in 20 or 50 or 100 years say about what all of you did for this country?"

1. How does President Obama hope that young people will respond to challenges?
   - (A) by living healthy lives
   - (B) by working hard to overcome obstacles
   - (C) by following the advice of adults
   - (D) by learning from history

2. What similarities do the three young people mentioned in the speech have?
   - (A) They all have challenges in their families and home lives.
   - (B) They all struggle to perform well in school.
   - (C) They all overcame adversity by setting and reaching goals.
   - (D) They all avoided adversity by making good decisions.

3. In what way does President Obama encourage young people to find success?
   - (A) He lays out a plan for financial success.
   - (B) He encourages them to ask lots of questions.
   - (C) He tells the students to only put their energy into things they enjoy.
   - (D) He encourages them to learn from failure.

4. What is a theme of the passage?
   - (A) Failure is inevitable.
   - (B) The key to success is perseverance.
   - (C) Young people should learn from history.
   - (D) Young people must expand their worldviews.

5. President Obama makes a connection between a student's future and his or her
   - (A) family.
   - (B) travels.
   - (C) intelligence.
   - (D) education.

6. What is the intended effect of the speech's tone on the audience?

   (A) The earnest tone is intended to inspire the audience.

   (B) The lighthearted tone is intended to entertain the audience.

   (C) The serious tone is intended to caution the audience.

   (D) The excited tone is meant to recruit the young audience.

7. Read this excerpt from President John F. Kennedy's speech proposing the Peace Corps to a group of university students in 1960.

   "How many of you who are going to be doctors, are willing to spend your days in Ghana? Technicians or engineers, how many of you are willing to work in the Foreign Service and spend your lives traveling around the world? On your willingness to do that, not merely to serve one year or two years in the service, but on your willingness to contribute part of your life to this country, I think will depend the answer whether a free society can compete. I think it can! And I think Americans are willing to contribute. But the effort must be far greater than we have ever made in the past."

   What theme do the two speeches have in common?

   (A) the power of overcoming failures to find success

   (B) the impact of young people on the future of America

   (C) the need for young people to to receive character education

   (D) the increasing difficulties for young people in America

Passage 2: "What Was the Space Shuttle?"
from *Nasa Knows* by Sandra May (2017)

1   The space shuttle was NASA's space transportation system. It carried astronauts and cargo to and from Earth's orbit. The first space shuttle flight took place April 12, 1981. The shuttle made its final landing July 21, 2011. During those 30 years, the space shuttle launched 135 missions.

What Did the Space Shuttle Do?
2   The space shuttle carried as many as seven astronauts at a time to and from space. In all, 355 people flew on the shuttle. Some of them flew more than one time. During its history, the space shuttle flew many different types of missions. It launched satellites and served as an orbiting science laboratory. Its crews repaired and improved other spacecraft, such as the Hubble Space Telescope. The shuttle also flew missions for the military. On its later missions, the space shuttle was mostly used to work on the International Space Station.

What Were the Parts of the Space Shuttle?
3   The space shuttle had three main parts. The first part was the orbiter. The orbiter was the large, white space plane where the crew lived and worked. It was the only part of the shuttle that flew into orbit. The orbiter also had a payload bay for carrying cargo into orbit. Five different orbiters took turns flying into space. The second part of the shuttle was the external tank. This was the large orange fuel tank that was attached to the bottom of the orbiter for launch. The third part was actually two pieces. A pair of white solid rocket boosters provided most of the thrust for the first two minutes of a shuttle launch. The solid rocket boosters were long and thin.

How Did the Space Shuttle Launch and Land?
4   The space shuttle took off like a rocket. The solid rocket boosters and the main engines on the orbiter provided the thrust, or push, for launch. The solid rocket boosters burned for about two minutes. Then the boosters dropped from the shuttle and fell into the ocean. Special boats brought them back so they could be used again. The shuttle's main engines fired for another six minutes. The external tank dropped off the orbiter and then burned up in Earth's atmosphere. At this point, the shuttle and its crew were in orbit.

5   The orbiter landed like a glider. While in orbit, it fired its engines to slow down. After re-entering Earth's atmosphere, it glided in for a landing on a runway. When the orbiter touched down on the runway, a parachute opened to help slow it down.

Where Are the Orbiters Now?
6   NASA had been using three orbiters when the space shuttle program stopped. They were Discovery, Atlantis and Endeavour. These three orbiters are now in museums for the public to

see. Discovery is on display at the Smithsonian's Steven F. Udvar-Hazy Center, in Chantilly, Va. Atlantis is at Kennedy Space Center's Visitor Complex in Florida. The California Science Center in Los Angeles is Endeavour's new home. During the shuttle program, two orbiters, Columbia and Challenger, were lost due to accidents. One other orbiter, Enterprise, never flew into space. It was built to test how the orbiters would work and is on display in New York City at the Intrepid Sea, Air & Space Museum.

8. Which of the following best describes a **main** function of the orbiter?
    - Ⓐ to house the crew in orbit
    - Ⓑ to fuel the space shuttle
    - Ⓒ to thrust the shuttle launch into orbit
    - Ⓓ to land smoothly

9. The shuttle was able to launch because of:
    - Ⓐ the Hubble Space Telescope
    - Ⓑ boosters falling into the ocean
    - Ⓒ gliding orbiters
    - Ⓓ thrust from engine boosters and engines

10. Which of the following sentences should be included in an objective summary of the article?
    - Ⓐ The space shuttle slowed down before landing.
    - Ⓑ Parts of the space shuttle now live at museums.
    - Ⓒ The space shuttle flew important missions for over 30 years.
    - Ⓓ The space shuttle was amazing!

11. How does the author explain the space shuttle's purpose over time?
    - Ⓐ It was the first equipment to orbit in space.
    - Ⓑ It had many jobs but eventually was used to repair other space equipment.
    - Ⓒ It flew the most missions to the moon.
    - Ⓓ It served as space transportation for many different countries.

12. How does the section "What Did the Space Shuttle Do?" (paragraph 2) contribute to the development of ideas in the article?
    - Ⓐ It explains why the space shuttle was an important part of the space program.
    - Ⓑ It reveals how the space shuttle functioned mechanically.
    - Ⓒ It provides an overall background of the space shuttle.
    - Ⓓ It tells an interesting story about a space mission to hook the reader.

13. What detail from the text supports the claim that the space shuttle helped other space innovations?

    (A) After re-entering Earth's atmosphere, the shuttle landed on a runway.

    (B) It repaired other spacecraft like the Hubble Space Telescope.

    (C) NASA used three orbiters before the shuttle was retired.

    (D) The Enterprise was built to test how other orbiters would work.

14. Examine the picture of a space shuttle orbiter.

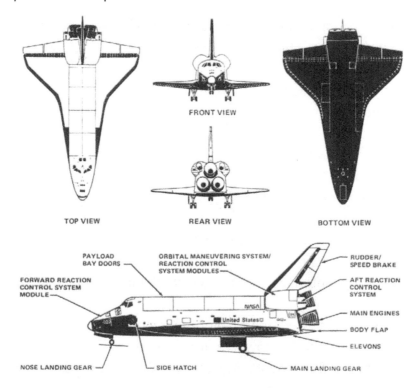

How does the image expand upon the information in the article?

    (A) It conflicts with the article's claim that the oribter lands smoothly.

    (B) It gives readers a better understanding of how astronauts live and work in the orbiter.

    (C) It provides a diagram that explains launch.

    (D) The diagram explains the parts and functions of the oribter.

Passage 3: Excerpt from *Narrative of the Life of Frederick Douglass, An American Slave*
by Frederick Douglass

1   My master's family consisted of two sons, Andrew and Richard; one daughter, Lucretia, and her husband, Captain Thomas Auld. They lived in one house, upon the home plantation of Colonel Edward Lloyd. My master was Colonel Lloyd's clerk and superintendent. He was what might be called the overseer of the overseers. I spent two years of childhood on this plantation in my old master's family. It was here that I witnessed the bloody transaction recorded in the first chapter; and as I received my first impressions of slavery on this plantation, I will give some description of it, and of slavery as it there existed. The plantation is about twelve miles north of Easton, in Talbot county, and is situated on the border of Miles River. The principal products raised upon it were tobacco, corn, and wheat. These were raised in great abundance; so that, with the products of this and the other farms belonging to him, he was able to keep in almost constant employment a large sloop, in carrying them to market at Baltimore. This sloop was named Sally Lloyd, in honor of one of the colonel's daughters. My master's son-in-law, Captain Auld, was master of the vessel; she was otherwise manned by the colonel's own slaves. Their names were Peter, Isaac, Rich, and Jake. These were **esteemed** very highly by the other slaves, and looked upon as the privileged ones of the plantation; for it was no small affair, in the eyes of the slaves, to be allowed to see Baltimore.

> principal = major, main
> overseer = a man in charge of slaves on a plantation
> transaction = event

2   Colonel Lloyd kept from three to four hundred slaves on his home plantation, and owned a large number more on the neighboring farms belonging to him. The names of the farms nearest to the home plantation were Wye Town and New Design. "Wye Town" was under the overseership of a man named Noah Willis. New Design was under the overseership of a Mr. Townsend. The overseers of these, and all the rest of the farms, numbering over twenty, received advice and direction from the managers of the home plantation. This was the great business place. It was the seat of government for the whole twenty farms. All disputes among the overseers were settled here. If a slave was convicted of any high misdemeanor, became unmanageable, or evinced a determination to run away, he was brought immediately here, severely whipped, put on board the sloop, carried to Baltimore, and sold to Austin Woolfolk, or some other slave-trader, as a warning to the slaves remaining.

3   Here, too, the slaves of all the other farms received their monthly allowance of food, and their yearly clothing. The men and women slaves received, as their monthly allowance

of food, eight pounds of pork, or its equivalent in fish, and one bushel of corn meal. Their yearly clothing consisted of two coarse linen shirts, one pair of linen trousers, like the shirts, one jacket, one pair of trousers for winter, made of coarse negro cloth, one pair of stockings, and one pair of shoes; the whole of which could not have cost more than seven dollars. The allowance of the slave children was given to their mothers, or the old women having the care of them. The children unable to work in the field had neither shoes, stockings, jackets, nor trousers, given to them; their clothing consisted of two coarse linen shirts per year. When these failed them, they went naked until the next allowance-day. Children from seven to ten years old, of both sexes, almost naked, might be seen at all seasons of the year.

4   There were no beds given the slaves, unless one coarse blanket be considered such, and none but the men and women had these. This, however, is not considered a very great [hardship]. They find less difficulty from the want of beds, than from the want of time to sleep; for when their day's work in the field is done, the most of them having their washing, mending, and cooking to do, and having few or none of the ordinary facilities for doing either of these, very many of their sleeping hours are consumed in preparing for the field the coming day; and when this is done, old and young, male and female, married and single, drop down side by side, on one common bed,—the cold, damp floor,—each covering himself or herself with their miserable blankets; and here they sleep till they are summoned to the field by the driver's horn. At the sound of this, all must rise, and be off to the field. There must be no halting; every one must be at his or her post; and woe betides them who hear not this morning summons to the field; for if they are not awakened by the sense of hearing, they are by the sense of feeling: no age nor [gender] finds any favor. Mr. Severe, the overseer, used to stand by the door of the quarter, armed with a large hickory stick and heavy cowskin, ready to whip any one who was so unfortunate as not to hear, or, from any other cause, was prevented from being ready to start for the field at the sound of the horn.

facilities = equipment
summoned = called
cowskin = the dried up hide of a cow cut in a strip and used as a whip

5   Mr. Severe was rightly named: he was a cruel man. I have seen him whip a woman, causing the blood to run half an hour at the time; and this, too, in the midst of her crying children, pleading for their mother's release. He seemed to take pleasure in... fiendish barbarity. Added to his cruelty, he was a profane swearer. It was enough to chill the blood and stiffen the hair of an ordinary man to hear him talk... The field was the place to witness his cruelty and profanity. His presence made it both the field of blood and of blasphemy. From the rising till the going down of the sun, he was cursing, raving, cutting, and slashing among the slaves of the field, in the most frightful manner. His career was short. He died very soon after I went to Colonel Lloyd's; and he died as he lived, uttering, with his dying groans, bitter curses and horrid oaths. His death was regarded by the slaves as the result of a merciful providence.

fiendish = cruel
barbarity = extreme brutality
profane = using curse words
blasphemy = speaking disrespectfully about God
merciful providence = protection and favor provided by God

15. Mr. Severe's attitude towards the slaves was:
    Ⓐ more compassionate to women than men.
    Ⓑ angered by those who didn't show loyalty.
    Ⓒ cruel to all.
    Ⓓ helpful.

16. Which is the most reasonable inference about the plantation based on paragraphs 1-2?
    Ⓐ It was a well-run, successful operation.
    Ⓑ It was so big that it became disorganized.
    Ⓒ It was organized by the Colonel's family.
    Ⓓ It was seen as the worst place to live.

17. Which phrase from the text helps the reader to understand the word "esteemed" as it is used in paragraph 1?
    Ⓐ "master of the vessel"
    Ⓑ "very highly by the other slaves"
    Ⓒ "raised in great abundance"
    Ⓓ "home plantation"

18. What is a theme of this text?
    Ⓐ Anger can ruin your life.
    Ⓑ Slaves deserve justice.
    Ⓒ Family is more important than anything.
    Ⓓ Kindness is contagious.

19. In paragraph 5, what does Douglass compare Mr. Severe's profanity and harsh words to?
    Ⓐ stress
    Ⓑ physical punishment
    Ⓒ slave rules
    Ⓓ curse words

20. Look at this painting titled "The Kneeling Slave, 'Am I not a man and a brother?'"

What message do both the text and this image convey?
- (A) Slaves felt chained by their masters.
- (B) It was very hot on most slave plantations.
- (C) Slaves often did not know their brothers.
- (D) Slaves had hope of one day escaping.

21. The reader can infer that the author feels the slaves were treated like
- (A) family.
- (B) employees.
- (C) animals.
- (D) children.

Passage 4: Excerpt from Alice's Adventures in Wonderland
by Lewis Carroll

1   Alice was beginning to get very tired of sitting by her sister on the bank, and of having nothing to do. Once or twice she had peeped into the book her sister was reading, but it had no pictures or conversations in it, "and what is the use of a book," thought Alice, "without pictures or conversations?"

2   So she was considering in her own mind (as well as she could, for the day made her feel very sleepy and stupid), whether the pleasure of making a daisy-chain would be worth the trouble of getting up and picking the daisies, when suddenly a White Rabbit with pink eyes ran close by her.

3   There was nothing so very remarkable in that, nor did Alice think it so very much out of the way to hear the Rabbit say to itself, "Oh dear! Oh dear! I shall be too late!" But when the Rabbit actually took a watch out of its waistcoat-pocket and looked at it and then hurried on, Alice started to her feet, for it flashed across her mind that she had never before seen a rabbit with either a waistcoat-pocket, or a watch to take out of it, and, burning with curiosity, she ran across the field after it and was just in time to see it pop down a large rabbit-hole, under the hedge. In another moment, down went Alice after it!

4   The rabbit-hole went straight on like a tunnel for some way and then dipped suddenly down, so suddenly that Alice had not a moment to think about stopping herself before she found herself falling down what seemed to be a very deep well.

5   Either the well was very deep, or she fell very slowly, for she had plenty of time, as she went down, to look about her. First, she tried to make out what she was coming to, but it was too dark to see anything; then she looked at the sides of the well and noticed that they were filled with cupboards and book-shelves; here and there she saw maps and pictures hung upon pegs. She took down a jar from one of the shelves as she passed. It was labeled "ORANGE MARMALADE," but, to her great disappointment, it was empty; she did not like to drop the jar, so managed to put it into one of the cupboards as she fell past it.

6   Down, down, down! Would the fall never come to an end? There was nothing else to do, so Alice soon began talking to herself. "Dinah'll miss me very much tonight, I should think!" (Dinah was the cat.) "I hope they'll remember her saucer of milk at tea-time. Dinah, my dear, I wish you were down here with me!" Alice felt that she was dozing off, when suddenly, thump! thump! down she came upon a heap of sticks and dry leaves, and the fall was over.

7   Alice was not a bit hurt, and she jumped up in a moment. She looked up, but it was all dark overhead; before her was another long passage and the White Rabbit was still in sight, hurrying down it. There was not a moment to be lost. Away went Alice like the wind and was just in time to hear it say, as it turned a corner, "Oh, my ears and whiskers, how late it's getting!" She was close behind it when she turned the corner, but the Rabbit was no longer to be seen.

22. In paragraph 3 what does the sentence "Oh dear! Oh dear! I shall be too late!" suggest?

    (A) The Rabbit is trying to attract attention.

    (B) Unlike Alice, the Rabbit is in a rush.

    (C) The Rabbit is trying to lure Alice to follow him.

    (D) Like Alice, the Rabbit is tired.

23. What does the word "remarkable" mean as it is used in paragraph 3?

    (A) chronic

    (B) open

    (C) notable

    (D) common

24. Read this phrase from paragraph 3. "...nor did Alice think it so very much out of the way to hear the Rabbit say..." What does the phrase suggest about Alice?

    (A) Alice is easily tricked into following the Rabbit.

    (B) She is innocent enough not to be startled by a talking Rabbit.

    (C) Alice feels guilty for leaving her sister.

    (D) She is shocked by the fact that the Rabbit can talk.

25. Information from the passage mostly likely suggests that

    (A) the Rabbit is likely to become a friend of Alice.

    (B) Alice is terrified in the rabbit hole.

    (C) Alice is looking back to retell the story from her perspective.

    (D) Alice is dreaming.

26. What is the effect of the phrase "thump! thump!" as it is used in paragraph 6?

    (A) It serves as a transition into the climax of the story.

    (B) The exclamatory phrase frightens the reader.

    (C) The repetition of the word "thump" alerts the reader that it is a key event in the story.

    (D) "Thump" is a sensory detail that emphasizes how Alice is jolted awake.

27. Which statement best states a theme of the story?

    (A) Being gullible can get you into a jam.

    (B) You can't judge a book by its cover.

    (C) The innocence of childhood is magical.

    (D) Seeking truth is necessary for survival.

28. What does the phrase "burning with curiosity" in paragraph 3 suggest about Alice?

    (A) She is so overcome with interest that she doesn't pause to consider the consequences.

    (B) She is put to sleep by the hot sun, causing her to seek shelter in the rabbit hole.

    (C) She can't wait to know what exciting adventure the rabbit is late for.

    (D) She is not concerned with the fact that the rabbit can speak.

Passage 5: Excerpt from *Little Men*
by Louisa May Alcott

CHAPTER I. NAT

1   "Please, sir, is this Plumfield?" asked a ragged boy of the man who opened the great gate at which the omnibus left him.

2   "Yes. Who sent you?"

3   "Mr. Laurence. I have got a letter for the lady."

4   "All right; go up to the house, and give it to her; she'll see to you, little chap."

5   The man spoke pleasantly, and the boy went on, feeling much cheered by the words. Through the soft spring rain that fell on sprouting grass and budding trees, Nat saw a large square house before him, a hospitable-looking house, with an old-fashioned porch, wide steps, and lights shining in many windows. Neither curtains nor shutters hid the cheerful glimmer; and, pausing a moment before he rang, Nat saw many little shadows dancing on the walls, heard the pleasant hum of young voices, and felt that it was hardly possible that the light and warmth and comfort within could be for a homeless "little chap" like him.

6   "I hope the lady will see to me," he thought, and gave a timid rap with the great bronze knocker, which was a jovial griffin's head.

7   A rosy-faced servant-maid opened the door, and smiled as she took the letter which he silently offered. She seemed used to receiving strange boys, for she pointed to a seat in the hall, and said, with a nod:

8   "Sit there and drip on the mat a bit, while I take this in to missis."

9   Nat found plenty to amuse him while he waited, and stared about him curiously, enjoying the view, yet glad to do so unobserved in the dusky recess by the door.

10   The house seemed swarming with boys, who were beguiling the rainy twilight with all sorts of amusements. There were boys everywhere, "up-stairs and down-stairs and in the lady's chamber," apparently, for various open doors showed pleasant groups of big boys, little boys, and middle-sized boys in all stages of evening relaxation, not to say effervescence. Two large rooms on the right were evidently schoolrooms, for desks, maps, blackboards, and books were scattered about. An open fire burned on the hearth, and several indolent lads lay on their backs before it, discussing a new cricket-ground, with such animation that their boots waved in the air. A tall youth was practising on the flute in one corner, quite undisturbed by the racket all about him. Two or three others were jumping over the desks, pausing, now and then, to get their breath and laugh at the droll sketches of a little wag who was caricaturing the whole household on a blackboard.

beguiling= charming
effervescence= enthusiasm
indolent- lazy
wag- jokester

11   In the room on the left a long supper-table was seen, set forth with great pitchers of new milk, piles of brown and white bread, and perfect stacks of the shiny gingerbread so dear to boyish souls. A flavor of toast was in the air, also suggestions of baked apples, very tantalizing to one hungry little nose and stomach.

12   The hall, however, presented the most inviting prospect of all, for a brisk game of tag was going on in the upper entry. One landing was devoted to marbles, the other to checkers, while the stairs were occupied by a boy reading, a girl singing a lullaby to her doll, two puppies, a kitten, and a constant succession of small boys sliding down the banisters, to the great detriment of their clothes and danger to their limbs.

13   So absorbed did Nat become in this exciting race, that he ventured farther and farther out of his corner; and when one very lively boy came down so swiftly that he could not stop himself, but fell off the banisters, with a crash that would have broken any head but one rendered nearly as hard as a cannon-ball by eleven years of constant bumping, Nat forgot himself, and ran up to the fallen rider, expecting to find him half-dead. The boy, however, only winked rapidly for a second, then lay calmly looking up at the new face with a surprised, "Hullo!"

14   "Hullo!" returned Nat, not knowing what else to say, and thinking that form of reply both brief and easy.

15   "Are you a new boy?" asked the recumbent youth, without stirring.

16   "Don't know yet."

17   "What's your name?"

18   "Nat Blake."

19   "Mine's Tommy Bangs. Come up and have a go, will you?" and Tommy got upon his legs like one suddenly remembering the duties of hospitality.

20   "Guess I won't, till I see whether I'm going to stay or not," returned Nat, feeling the desire to stay increase every moment.

21 "I say, Demi, here's a new one. Come and see to him;" and the lively Thomas returned to his sport with unabated relish.

> relish= enjoyment

22   At his call, the boy reading on the stairs looked up with a pair of big brown eyes, and after an instant's pause, as if a little shy, he put the book under his arm, and came soberly down to greet the new-comer, who found something very attractive in the pleasant face of this slender, mild-eyed boy.

23   "Have you seen Aunt Jo?" he asked, as if that was some sort of important ceremony.

24   "I haven't seen anybody yet but you boys; I'm waiting," answered Nat.

25   "Did Uncle Laurie send you?" proceeded Demi, politely, but gravely.

26   "Mr. Laurence did."

27   "He is Uncle Laurie; and he always sends nice boys."

28   Nat looked gratified at the remark, and smiled, in a way that made his thin face very pleasant. He did not know what to say next, so the two stood staring at one another in friendly silence, till the little girl came up with her doll in her arms. She was very like Demi, only not so tall, and had a rounder, rosier face, and blue eyes.

29   "This is my sister, Daisy," announced Demi, as if presenting a rare and precious creature.

30   The children nodded to one another; and the little girl's face dimpled with pleasure, as she said affably:

31   "I hope you'll stay. We have such good times here; don't we, Demi?"

32   "Of course, we do: that's what Aunt Jo has Plumfield for."

33   "It seems a very nice place indeed," observed Nat, feeling that he must respond to these amiable young persons.

34   "It's the nicest place in the world, isn't it, Demi?" said Daisy, who evidently regarded her brother as authority on all subjects.

35   "No, I think Greenland, where the icebergs and seals are, is more interesting. But I'm fond of Plumfield, and it is a very nice place to be in," returned Demi, who was interested just now in a book on Greenland. He was about to offer to show Nat the pictures and explain them, when the servant returned, saying with a nod toward the parlor-door:

36   "All right; you are to stop."

37   "I'm glad; now come to Aunt Jo." And Daisy took him by the hand with a pretty protecting air, which made Nat feel at home at once.

38   Demi returned to his beloved book, while his sister led the new-comer into a back room, where a stout gentleman was frolicking with two little boys on the sofa, and a thin lady was just finishing the letter which she seemed to have been re-reading.

39   "Here he is, aunty!" cried Daisy.

40   "So this is my new boy? I am glad to see you, my dear, and hope you'll be happy here," said the lady, drawing him to her, and stroking back the hair from his forehead with a kind hand and a motherly look, which made Nat's lonely little heart yearn toward her.

41   She was not at all handsome, but she had a merry sort of face that never seemed to have forgotten certain childish ways and looks, any more than her voice and manner had; and these things, hard to describe but very plain to see and feel, made her a genial, comfortable kind of person, easy to get on with, and generally "jolly," as boys would say. She saw the little tremble of Nat's lips as she smoothed his hair, and her keen eyes grew softer, but she only drew the shabby figure nearer and said, laughing:

42   "I am Mother Bhaer, that gentleman is Father Bhaer, and these are the two little Bhaers. Come here, boys, and see Nat."

29. Read this phrase from a sentence from the text.
   "So this is my new boy? I am glad to see you, my dear, and hope you'll be happy..."
   What does the sentence suggest about Aunt Jo?
   - (A) It reveals that she is fair.
   - (B) It helps the reader see her as kind and motherly.
   - (C) It helps the reader understand why Nat is uneasy.
   - (D) It reveals that she is related to Nat.

30. What does the point of view in paragraph 23 help the reader to understand?
   (A) that the home at Plumfield is very ceremonious
   (B) that Nat will fit in at Plumfield immediately
   (C) that they boys at Plumfield are shy and hesitant
   (D) that Aunt Jo is an important figure at Plumfield

31. What event in the story **first** helps Nat understand that he has a place in the home.
   (A) Daisy takes him by the hand.
   (B) Nat is given a letter.
   (C) Demi explains all he knows about Greenland to Nat.
   (D) Nat knocks shyly on the front door.

32. Which of the following words **best** replaces "frolicking" from paragraph 38 in the text?
   (A) running
   (B) arguing
   (C) horseplaying
   (D) following

33. What is the most likely reason the author chose to tell this story in a third person point of view?
   (A) to provide information about Nat's early life
   (B) to explain that Plumfield is an expensive place to live
   (C) to provide Nat's thoughts, and to provide objective observations about Plumfield
   (D) to show that Nat immediately feels at home in Aunt Jo's presence

34. Which sentence best states a theme of the excerpt?
   (A) All children deserve warmth and comfort.
   (B) Education is a passageway to greater learning.
   (C) Structure is the key to success.
   (D) Grief and loss makes a person kinder.

35. What can the reader infer about Plumfield from paragraph 5?
   (A) It is unlikely to be a permanent home for Nat.
   (B) It is in the heart of the woods.
   (C) It is cheerful and welcoming.
   (D) It is fancy and proper.

NY STATE STANDARDS ASSESSMENT

ELA
Practice Test One

Session One

Answer Key &
Explanations

Passage 1: "President Obama's National Address to America's Schoolchildren" (Excerpt)

1. **B.** President Obama's speech encourages students to work hard through adversity, giving examples of other young people who have found success this way. **Standard RI.5.1**

2. **C.** This is the only correct answer that all three young people have in common, as each experienced hardship but overcame it to find success. D is incorrect because the young people experienced adversity, though not typically because of poor decisions. **Standard RI.5.3**

3. **D.** President Obama encourages people to find success by learning from failure. Answer choice B is a strong distractor because he does encourage students to seek help, however, his main point is that to be successful one must overcome failure. **Standard RI.5.2**

4. **B.** Theme is a main idea or underlying meaning of a literary work that may be stated directly or indirectly. In this speech the themes are stated directly, focusing on the ability to find success through commitment to overcoming obstacles. **Standard RI.5.2**

5. **D.** This question identifies the reader's ability to see the relationship between two ideas. President Obama makes the connection between a bright future and education by introducing the need for setting goals in education in paragraph 8 and elaborating through the remainder of the speech on how that leads to success. **Standard RI.5.3**

6. **A.** Tone reflects what the author wants the reader to take away. The tone of the speech is intended to inspire the audience. C is a strong distractor, but incorrect because though the speech is serious, the intent is to inspire, not caution the audience. **Standard RI.5.6**

7. **B.** President Kennedy's speech is a clear call for young people to give of themselves in service to the Peace Corps, saying that free society (democracy) counts on Americans being willing to contribute. President Obama's speech is less straightforward, but paragraphs 16-17 draw the connection between young people being willing to stand up for democratic beliefs, while paragraph 18 challenges young people, asking what a future president will say they did for the country. **Standard RI.5.9**

Passage 2: "What Was the Space Shuttle?"
8. **A.** The oribter is where an astronaut crew lives and works in space (paragraph 3). The other answer choices are incorrect. **Standard RI.5.1**

9. **D.** Paragraph 4 explains that the space shuttle launched due to thrust from the engines and boosters, showing the relationship between parts and their functions. **Standard RI.5.3**

10. **C.** An objective summary states primarily main ideas and potentially a few supporting details of the passage. One main idea is that the space shuttle performed many tasks and missions over a 30-year period. Answer choices A and B are not central ideas, only supporting details. An objective summary does not just contain a supporting detail. Answer choice D is not an objective statement. **Standard RI.5.2**

11. **B.** Over time, the space shuttle served many functions. It was transportation for astronauts (but not many countries, as answer choice D suggests), and helped repair space equipment like the International Space Station and Hubble Space Telescope (paragraph 2). The other answers (A and C) are not supported by any evidence in the text. **Standard RI.5.3**

12. **A.** Paragraph 2 sets the stage for understanding the purpose of the space shuttle by providing background information about its purpose and duties. **Standard RI.5.5**

13. **B.** To answer this question, students must both make an inference based on information in the text, and use evidence to support that inference. Because paragraph 2 mentions the space shuttle was used to make repairs, the reader can infer that the space shuttle furthered other space innovations. **Standard RI.5.8**

14. **D.** The diagram of the orbiter provides more information about the structure and functions of the oribter, expanding on information in the article. **Standard RI.5.7**

Passage 3: *Narrative of the Life of Frederick Douglass, An American Slave* (Excerpt)

15. **C.** Mr. Severe was cruel to the slaves in his care. He beat them and cursed at them. No other answer choice captures Mr. Severe's attitude toward the slave. **Standard RI.5.3**

16. **A.** The plantation ran like an organized business, stated in paragraph 2. The reader may be tricked by answer choice D, but nothing in the text leads the reader to infer that the plantation was the worst place to live. In paragraph 4 Douglass even states that the accommodation (or lack of) was not seen

as a hardship. Answer choice C may also seem reasonable, however close reading of paragraph 1 indicates that the plantation was run and organized by the Colonel's clerk and superintendent. **Standard RI.5.1**

17. **B.** The word "esteemed" most nearly means "respected" or "admired." Context clues in the text lead the reader to understand its meaning, specifically that these slaves were looked at "highly" by other slaves. **Standard RI.5.4**

18. **B.** The theme of the text is that slaves deserve justice. This becomes evident in the final paragraph, where the slaves view it as God's favor when Mr. Severe dies after being so cruel to them. They felt they received justice. **Standard RI.5.2**

19. **B.** Douglass says that Mr. Severe's language was "profane." He links the master's profanity and cruelty by discussing them in parallel. Douglass seems to equate physical and verbal punishment as equally harmful. **Standard RI.5.6**

20. **A.** The image shows a slave, kneeling and in chains, asking a question of whether he is also a rightful citizen. This supports the text's claim that slaves felt chained, both physically and metaphorically. **Standard RI.5.7**

21. **C.** Douglass insinuates that the slave workers were treated closely to animals, the plantation a farm that simply used the slaves as labor. Choices A and B are incorrect, because though the slaves were paid a small amount, they were treated inhumanely and worked to the bone. **Standard RI.5.6**

Passage 4: *Alice's Adventures in Wonderland* (Excerpt)
22. **B.** In the story, the Rabbit is clearly in a hurry, based on this sentence and the context of looking at his watch. B is further correct because the events indicate that Alice is not in a hurry, contrasting their actions. **Standard RL.5.3**

23. **C.** The word "remarkable" is used to indicate that there was nothing out of the ordinary to Alice about the Rabbit with pink eyes running by here. "Remarkable" can best be replaced with the word "notable," indicating something unusual. **Standard RL.5.4**

24. **B.** The phrase indicates that Alice is childlike in her innocence that she would not be startled by a talking Rabbit. The Rabbit does not try to trick her, not even acknowledging her presence, therefore answer choice A is incorrect. **Standard RL.5.3**

25. **D.** This question asks for the reader to infer an answer based on the context of the text. Choice D is the most likely response, because the text includes many dream-like features, including Alice floating slowly down the hole, the talking Rabbit, etc.. **Standard RL.5.1**

26. **D.** The phrase "thump! thump!" is an example of onomatopoeia, a stylistic choice the writer makes in order to show how Alice is awakened after nearly falling asleep. Choice C mentions the repetition, which is also a literary device, but is incorrect because this instance is not a key event in the story. **Standard RL.5.5**

27. **C.** The story focuses on Alice's innocence. First, she is clearly unimpressed by her sister's "adult" book, lacking pictures. She spontaneously follows a talking Rabbit, and drifts, dream-like down a rabbit hole. Therefore, the reader can infer that the author's message revolves around the innocence of childhood. **Standard RL.5.2**

28. **A.** This phrase helps characterize Alice as spontaneous and unhindered by time. She immediately decided to find out more about the mysterious talking Rabbit, following him down his hole. C is not the best answer because Alice seems concerned only with following the strange rabbit, and does not think or ask what he is late for. **Standard RL.5.3**

Passage 5: *Little Men* (Excerpt)
29. **B.** This question asks the reader to infer something about Aunt Jo's character based on the text. Aunt Jo's dialogue shows that she is kind to Nat, and that she acts with motherly love, welcoming him. The reader might have difficulty choosing between A and B, but the text more closely implies that Jo is kind, rather than fair. **Standard RL.5.3**

30. **D.** This question asks the reader to identify how the narrator's point of view impacts the reader's understanding. This paragraph establishes Aunt Jo's importance, stating that meeting her seems like some sort of ceremony. **Standard RL.5.6**

31. **A.** This question asks for the event which first allows Nat to feel he is at home. Paragraph 37 states that, "... Daisy took him by the hand with a pretty protecting air, which made Nat feel at home at once." This is the first place in the text that the narrator mentions Nat feeling like he belongs at Plumfield. Though Choice C does occur, the narrator does not offer any clue as to Nat's feelings of belonging at Demi's Greenland explanation. **Standard RL.5.5**

32. **C.** The word "frolicking" as used in paragraph 38 most nearly means that the gentleman was playing around, or horseplaying, with the boys. Frolicking can also mean running, however in the context of this text, horseplaying is a better replacement. **Standard RL.5.4**

33. **C.** The narrator of the text is third person omniscient, meaning he or she can both narrate events and the thoughts and feelings of others. This serves to give objective observations of Plumfield, but also to allow the reader to know Nat's thoughts and feelings. **Standard RL.5.6**

34. **A.** The theme, or author's message, in this text revolves around Nat, an orphan, deserving the warmth and comfort that Plumfield has to offer. At the beginning of the passage he states that a place like Plumfield isn't for an orphan like him, but the inhabitants of Plumfield show that he is indeed welcome. **Standard RL.5.2**

35. **C.** In paragraph 5 the narrator uses imagery related to spring (sprouting grass, budding trees) and comfort (lights, warmth). This imagery and word choice leads the reader to understand that Plumfield is cheerful and welcoming. **Standard RL.5.1**

NY STATE STANDARDS ASSESSMENT

ELA
Practice Test One

Session Two

Directions: Read this passage. Then answer questions 36-38.

Passage 6: Excerpt from *Peter Pan,* Chapter 15: Hook or Me This
by J.M. Barrie

1   ...When last we saw [Peter] he was stealing across the island with one finger to his lips and his dagger at the ready. He had seen the crocodile pass by without noticing anything peculiar about it, but by and by he remembered that it had not been ticking. At first he thought this eerie, but soon concluded rightly that the clock had run down.

eerie = spooky

2   Without giving a thought to what might be the feelings of a fellow-creature thus abruptly deprived of its closest companion, Peter began to consider how he could turn the catastrophe to his own use; and he decided to tick, so that wild beasts should believe he was the crocodile and let him pass [unharmed]. He ticked superbly, but with one unforeseen result. The crocodile was among those who heard the sound, and it followed him, though whether with the purpose of regaining what it had lost, or merely as a friend under the belief that it was again ticking itself, will never be certainly known, for, like slaves to a fixed idea, it was a stupid beast.

3   Peter reached the shore without mishap, and went straight on, his legs encountering the water as if quite unaware that they had entered a new element… As he swam he had but one thought: "Hook or me this time." He had ticked so long that he now went on ticking without knowing that he was doing it. Had he known he would have stopped, for to board the brig by help of the tick, though an ingenious idea, had not occurred to him.

mishap = issue or accident
brig = the area of a ship used as a jail
ingenious = smart

4   On the contrary, he thought he had scaled her side as noiseless as a mouse; and he was amazed to see the pirates cowering from him, with Hook in their midst as abject as if he had heard the crocodile.

5   The crocodile! No sooner did Peter remember it than he heard the ticking. At first he thought the sound did come from the crocodile, and he looked behind him swiftly. Then he realised that he was doing it himself, and in a flash he understood the situation. "How clever of me!" he thought at once, and signed to the boys not to burst into applause.

6   It was at this moment that Ed Teynte the quartermaster emerged from the forecastle and came along the deck. Now, reader, time what happened by your watch. Peter struck true

and deep. John clapped his hands on the ill-fated pirate's mouth to stifle the dying groan. He fell forward. Four boys caught him to prevent the thud. Peter gave the signal, and the carrion was cast overboard. There was a splash, and then silence. How long has it taken?

> forecastle = the upper deck of a ship
> carrion = deceased person

7   "One!" (Slightly had begun to count.)

8   None too soon, Peter, every inch of him on tiptoe, vanished into the cabin; for more than one pirate was screwing up his courage to look round. They could hear each other's distressed breathing now, which showed them that the more terrible sound had passed. "It's gone, captain," Smee said, wiping off his spectacles. "All's still again."

9   Slowly Hook let his head emerge from his ruff, and listened so intently that he could have caught the echo of the tick. There was not a sound, and he drew himself up firmly to his full height.

10   "Then here's to Johnny Plank!" he cried brazenly, hating the boys more than ever because they had seen him unbend. He broke into the villainous ditty:
"Yo ho, yo ho, the frisky plank,
You walks along it so,
Till it goes down and you goes down
To Davy Jones below!"

11   To terrorize the prisoners the more, though with a certain loss of dignity, he danced along an imaginary plank, grimacing at them as he sang; and when he finished he cried, "Do you want a touch of the cat [o' nine tails] before you walk the plank?"

12   At that they fell on their knees. "No, no!" they cried so piteously that every pirate smiled.

13   "Fetch the cat, Jukes," said Hook; "it's in the cabin."

> cat = a whip

14   The cabin! Peter was in the cabin! The children gazed at each other.

15   "Ay, ay," said Jukes blithely, and he strode into the cabin. They followed him with their eyes; they scarce knew that Hook had resumed his song...

16   What was the last line will never be known, for of a sudden the song was stayed by a dreadful screech from the cabin. It wailed through the ship, and died away. Then was heard a crowing sound which was well understood by the boys, but to the pirates was almost more eerie than the screech.

17 "What was that?" cried Hook.

18 "Two," said Slightly solemnly.

19 The Italian Cecco hesitated for a moment and then swung into the cabin. He tottered out, haggard.

20 "What's the matter with Bill Jukes, you dog?" hissed Hook, towering over him.

21 "The matter wi' him is he's dead, stabbed," replied Cecco in a hollow voice.

22 "Bill Jukes dead!" cried the startled pirates.

23 "The cabin's as black as a pit," Cecco said, almost gibbering, "but there is something terrible in there: the thing you heard crowing."

24 The exaltation of the boys, the lowering looks of the pirates, both were seen by Hook. "Cecco," he said in his most steely voice, "go back and fetch me out that doodle-doo." Cecco, bravest of the brave, cowered before his captain, crying "No, no"; but Hook was purring to his claw.

25 "Did you say you would go, Cecco?" he said musingly.

26 Cecco went, first flinging his arms despairingly. There was no more singing, all listened now; and again came a death-screech and again a crow.

27 No one spoke except Slightly. "Three," he said.

28 Hook rallied his dogs with a gesture. "'S'death and odds fish," he thundered, "who is to bring me that doodle-doo?"

29 "Wait till Cecco comes out," growled Starkey, and the others took up the cry.

30 "I think I heard you volunteer, Starkey," said Hook, purring again.

31 "No, by thunder!" Starkey cried.

32 "My hook thinks you did," said Hook, crossing to him. "I wonder if it would not be advisable, Starkey, to humour the hook?"

33 "I'll swing before I go in there," replied Starkey doggedly, and again he had the support of the crew.

34 "Is this mutiny?" asked Hook more pleasantly than ever. "Starkey's ringleader!"

> mutiny = a rebellion of the crew to take the ship from the ship's captain

35 "Captain, mercy!" Starkey whimpered, all of a tremble now.

36 "Shake hands, Starkey," said Hook, proffering his claw.

37 Starkey looked round for help, but all deserted him. As he backed up Hook advanced, and now the red spark was in his eye. With a despairing scream the pirate leapt upon Long Tom and precipitated himself into the sea.

38 "Four," said Slightly.

39 "And now," Hook said courteously, "did any other gentlemen say mutiny?" Seizing a lantern and raising his claw with a menacing gesture, "I'll bring out that doodle-doo myself," he said, and sped into the cabin.

40 "Five." How Slightly longed to say it. He wetted his lips to be ready, but Hook came staggering out, without his lantern.

41   "Something blew out the light," he said a little unsteadily.

36. How does Peter Pan use trickery to outsmart and fight the pirates? Use **two** details from the story to support your response.

_____

_____

_____

_____

_____

_____

_____

_____

_____

_____

_____

_____

37. What details from the story lead the reader to believe that Hook is not as brave as he pretends to be? Use **two** details from the story to support your response.

_____

_____

_____

_____

_____

_____

_____

_____

_____

38. In the passage, Slightly, one of Hook's prisoners, starts counting What effect does Slightly's counting have on the development of the plot? Use **two** details from the story to support your response.

_____

_____

_____

_____

_____

_____

_____

_____

_____

Passage 7: Our Foreigners (Extract)
by Samuel P. Orth

1   In 1820 there were 8385 immigrants who came to live in America, and nearly one half came from Ireland. By 1900 there were nearly five million persons in the United States who had arrived from Ireland.

2   Many immigrants, especially Catholics, left Ireland because the laws didn't give them the freedom to practice their religion.

3   Many immigrants also wanted to own land. According to one historian, the Irishman viewed "the right to have a bit of land exactly as other people regard the right to live."

4   However, the main of reason why immigrants felt forced to leave was because of the famine in Ireland. They couldn't find enough food to live. The potato crop failed. According to an Irish historian, the poorest Irish lived on the potato, and whole generations grew up, lived, married, and died without ever having tasted meat. Of course, this is an exaggeration, but it is true that potatoes are one of the main foods food for the Irish, so many years of potato crop failure was disastrous for them.

5   The potato rot in the cold and damp summer of 1845 followed by a two-year long plant disease destroyed the entire crop. As a result, two million Irish died from starvation and fever. There was simply not enough food to feed everyone. Many people became ill because their bodies were so weakened from not eating. Sadly, they were no longer strong enough to fight off the fever. Needless to say, this was a very sad time in Ireland.

6   This national disaster touched American hearts. Relief ships were sent across from America to help, and many a shipload of Irish peasants were brought back. In 1845 over 44,821 came; 1847 saw this number rise to 105,536 and in the next year to 112,934.

7   Yet, it is not true that Irish migration to the United States began after the great famine. In reality, it was only the climax. Long before this, in the 1600s, Irishmen had arrived in America to work and buy land; then, from 1775-1783, Irish-Americans came to America to fight in American wars; and then there was the Irish-American pioneers who settled in the Mississippi Valley. How many Irish there were in those days, we do not know, but we do know there were enough in Boston to celebrate St. Patrick's Day.

39. Why did many Irish immigrate to the United States? Use **two** details from the story to support your response.

_____

_____

_____

_____

_____

_____

_____

_____

_____

_____

_____

_____

_____

40. Where in the text does the author show evidence to support the claim that the potato famine was actually the climax, and not the beginning, of the Irish migration to America? Use **two** details from the story to support your response.

_____

_____

_____

_____

_____

_____

_____

_____

_____

_____

_____

_____

41. What details does the author provide to show the full picture of how the potato famine affected Irish citizens? Use **two** details from the story to support your response.

_____

_____

_____

_____

_____

_____

_____

_____

_____

_____

_____

_____

_____

_____

_____

_____

_____

_____

_____

_____

_____

_____

_____

_____

_____

_____

_____

_____

_____

Directions: Read this passage. Then answer question 42.

Passage 8: The Journal of Andrew Leary O'Brien (1837)
by Andrew Leary O'Brien

1   We started out to sea, and in twelve hours we lost sight of England, and then of the Lovely Green Isle of Ireland. Towards evening I felt sea-sick, and before night I was.

2   After two weeks at sea, a young woman who appeared to be sick from the start, died and was thrown overboard. This sight made my heart heavy, especially since the burial was done with very little concern. The death seemed to be scarcely noticed.

3   A committee was appointed in each cabin to ensure that the passengers kept themselves and everything else clean, under penalty of being deprived of their water allowance.

4   The Captain sent word that we must bury her. Being fully the Irishman, independent and wild, I sent word back by the mate that he, the Captain, may bury her. He concluded there was no use in bullying us. He sent the first mate and three sailors and they sewed up the dead woman in a sheet, with some rocks at her feet. All the Irish passengers knelt down and prayed earnestly for the dead, and when done, she was thrown overboard.

5   As we moved into sight of the New Jersey shores our anticipation rose—the white cottages on the Jersey shore called to us. The sight was beyond description. It was majestic and grand to us who had never witnessed the likes of it before.

6   As we got nearer, however, we were somewhat disappointed to see such a vast and wild forest. We concluded that the country was somewhat savage. We longed for our dear, sweet, familiar Ireland.

7   There were several aboard not well yet, and when we arrived at the place of quarantine, they were not allowed ashore. Those that were well were sent on by railroad.

8   When I was ashore on the streets of New York, I felt lightheaded with joy. When I attempted to walk, I raised my foot three times higher than necessary. I felt like I was walking on air. I was in New York, the city of dreams!

42. In "Excerpt from *Our Foreigners"* and *The Journal of Andrew Leary O'Brien,* how are the experiences of Irish immigrants represented? Use details from both texts to support your response.

In your response, be sure to
- explain how immigrants are described and represented in both passages
- compare these representations
- use details from both articles to support your response

NY STATE STANDARDS ASSESSMENT

ELA
Practice Test One

Session Two

Answer Key & Explanations

Passage 6: Peter Pan (Excerpt)

36. Answers will vary. Students can score between 0-2 points for short response answers. Peter shows his cleverness by imitating the tick of the crocodile and by crowing in the cabin, making the pirates think there is a rooster. The details that students use will vary, but some examples of the details that support this are:
• "Peter began to consider how he could turn the catastrophe to his own use; and he decided to tick, so that wild beasts should believe he was the crocodile and let him pass [unharmed]."
• "Then was heard a crowing sound which was well understood by the boys, but to the pirates was almost more eerie than the screech." **Standard RL.5.2**

37. **Answers will vary.** Students can score between 0-2 points for short response answers. Hook is clearly afraid of both the crocodile and the rooster, and seems to hate that the Lost Boys have seen his fright. The details that students use will vary, but some details that students use will vary, but some examples of the details that support this are:
• "Slowly Hook let his head emerge from his ruff, and listened so intently that he could have caught the echo of the tick."
• "'Then here's to Johnny Plank!' he cried brazenly, hating the boys more than ever because they had seen him unbend." **Standard RL.5.1**

38. **Answers will vary.** Students can score between 0-2 points for short response answers. Slightly's counting shows that Peter and the Lost Boys are outsmarting and overtaking the pirates. It also foreshadows that something may happen to Hook. The details that students use will vary, but some examples of the details that support this are:
• "'One!' (Slightly had begun to count.)"
• "'Five.' How Slightly longed to say it."
Standard RL.5.5

Passage 7: Our Foreigners (Excerpt)

39. Answers will vary. Students can score between 0-2 points for short response answers. Irish immigrated to America because of religious persecution, the pursuit of owning land, and because of the Irish famine. The details that students use will vary, but some examples of the details that support this are:
• "Many immigrants, especially Catholics, left Ireland because the laws didn't give them the freedom to practice their religion."
• "...Irishman viewed 'the right to have a bit of land exactly as other people regard the right to live.'"
• "They couldn't find enough food to live."
Standard RI.5.1

40. **Answers will vary.** Students can score between 0-2 points for short response answers. The author shows that the migration of Irish people to America began before the potato famine. The details that students use will vary, but some examples of the details that support this are:
• "Long before this, in the 1600s, Irishmen had arrived in America to work and buy land; then, from 1775-1783, Irish-Americans came to America to fight in American wars; and then there was the Irish-American pioneers who settled in the Mississippi Valley."
• "How many Irish there were in those days, we do not know, but we do know there were enough in Boston to celebrate St. Patrick's Day." **Standard RI.5.8**

41. **Answers will vary.** Students can score between 0-2 points for short response answers. The Irish potato famine affected many aspects of life for the Irish, especially the poorest citizens. The details that students use will vary, but some examples of the details that support this are:
• "They couldn't find enough food to live."
• "...the poorest Irish lived on the potato..."
• "Many people became ill because their bodies were so weakened from not eating." **Standard RI.5.1, RL.5.3**

Passage 8: The Journal of Andrew Leary O'Brien (1837)
42. **Answers will vary.** Students can score between 0-4 points for extended response answers. Students can use evidence from both sources to answer this question. For example: From Source 1:
• Immigrants were forced to seek a new life in America due to religious persecution, a desire to own land, and famine.
• Famine was a particularly dire cause of immigration, and was the climax of immigration to America for the Irish.
• Relief ships were sent from America to Ireland to collect poor peasants who might otherwise die from illness or starvation. From Source 2:
• Many immigrants on the ship to America were sick, some to the point of death.
• The immigrants were excited as they neared America, but homesick at the realization that it was different from Ireland.
• The author's exclamation of "New York, the city of dreams!" gives the sense that he seeks opportunity and is thrilled at the opportunity afforded him in the new world.

Example Student Response: In "Excerpt from Our Foreigners" and The Journal of Andrew Leary O'Brien the authors presents several ideas about the lives of Irish immigrants. "Excerpt from Our Foreigners" shows that Irish citizens, especially poor ones, suffered in Ireland in the 1800s, mostly due to a famine because the potato crop failed. This caused Americans to send ships to Ireland to collect poor, and sometimes sick, Irish people to bring to America.

The text also points out that many immigrants came before the famine, to seek religious freedom and to find land. This was different from those who were essentially forced to immigrate, or else die from illness or starvation.

In The Journal of Andrew Leary O'Brien the author recounts his experience on a ship to America, providing first-hand evidence of the illness experienced by recounting the death of a young woman on the ship. The journal entry provides the reader a chance to see how the immigrants felt--both excited at the coming to America, and also homesick for Ireland.

The final paragraph of the second passage, when the speaker exclaims his excitement at being in New York ("New York, the city of dreams!"), provides a first-hand account of the reasoning for immigrants who came seeking opportunity and freedom, as opposed to the sole reason of escaping famine. **Standard RI.5.1, RI.5.3, RI.5.9**

NY STATE STANDARDS ASSESSMENT

ELA
Practice Test Two

Session One

Passage 1: Sasha's Clean Room

1   Sasha couldn't wait to get home to play with her new slime that had received as a gift over the holidays. After returning to school for the first day after a fun Winter break, she was glad the wait was finally over. She could imagine her older brother reminding her that days of playing and having fun were over and they just had to go back to school again the next day, but she pushed the thought away. Nothing could stand in the way of playing with her new slime now that the school day was over.

2   She stared out the window as the bus turned onto her street. Just a little bit longer, she thought. Soon, the bus stopped, and the door opened to let her off.

3   "Have a great day," her bus driver called out.

4   "You too!" Sasha ran to the front door of her house and ran inside. "Hi, Mom," she said as she passed her mom sitting in the living room. "Hold on," her Mom said, but Sasha didn't hear her because she was already in the hall leading to her bedroom.

5   She quickly slammed the door and nearly tripped over the toys she'd left sitting out on her floor from the night before. She remembered her mom telling her yesterday to clean up before going to bed, but she had played with her slime instead.

6   She looked at the mess and thought maybe she should clean it before getting started. She knew her mother would be mad if she saw the mess. She saw her slime containers sitting on her desk, then looked at the mess again. If her mom found the mess, she'd probably lose some of her privileges, and her mom might confiscate her slime.

7   Sasha groaned as she quickly scooped up all her toys and tossed them into the closet. Now, the floor was clean. She closed the closet and opened her container of slime.

8   A moment later, her mother walked in. After glancing at the floor, a look of surprise came over her face. "Oh," she said. "You cleaned up."

9   Sasha kept her eyes focused on her slime. "Yep."

10   She sat down on the bed next to her. "Good day at school?" she asked as she looked around the room.

11   "I guess so," she replied, not looking away from the slime.

12   "I think it might be time to start taking some breaks from the break, don't you think?"

13   "Why, Mom?"

14 Her mom stood up and walked over to the closet and opened it. Several of the toys that Sasha had tossed in fell out. Sasha paused playing with her slime and looked at her mom. Disappointment was written all over her mom's face.

15 "This is why," she said.

16 She knew she'd let her mother down. "I'm sorry, Mom," she said, putting the slime away in the container. She spent the next thirty minutes cleaning up the right way, and when she was finished, she decided she could always play with her slime tomorrow and went to spend time with her mom instead.

1. What can the reader infer about Sasha's relationship with her mother?
   (A) Sasha's mother is mean, and she fears disobeying her.
   (B) Sasha's mother is nice, but Sasha has little respect for her.
   (C) Sasha's mother allows Sasha to do almost anything she wants.
   (D) Sasha loves her mother and doesn't want to disappoint her.

2. Which of the following best reflects the theme of the passage?
   (A) Putting off what your parents tell you to do is alright as long as you apologize for it.
   (B) We shouldn't let a focus on our own entertainment take all our attention away from other things that really matter.
   (C) Trust is lost when lies are told.
   (D) A clean room is better than playing with slime.

3. What can the reader infer about why Sasha chose to not play with her slime after she finally cleaned her room?
   (A) She got in trouble because of the slime, and she didn't want to get in trouble again.
   (B) She lost interest in playing with it while she was cleaning her room.
   (C) Her mother told her she couldn't play with it again until the next day.
   (D) She loved her mother and wanted to do what was right.

4. Which of the following definitions best matches the author's use of the word confiscate in Paragraph 6?
   (A) hide for fun
   (B) take away temporarily
   (C) use
   (D) criticize

5. Why does the author include the detail about Sasha's mother telling her to "hold on" in Paragraph 4?

    Ⓐ to hint that her mother wants to talk to her about something

    Ⓑ to show that her mother values talking to her when she first gets home

    Ⓒ to show that Sasha doesn't listen to her mother

    Ⓓ to show that Sasha needs to slow down when she's in the house

6. From whose point-of-view is the story told?

    Ⓐ the bus driver

    Ⓑ Sasha's older brother

    Ⓒ Sasha's mother

    Ⓓ Sasha

7. Which of the following image descriptions would most likely give the reader an idea of what her story is about?

    Ⓐ a school bus driving down the road

    Ⓑ a floor with toys spread all about

    Ⓒ a woman's angry face

    Ⓓ a girl buying a container of slime at a store

Passage 2 The Decision to Drop the Bomb
by USHistory.org

1   America had the bomb. Now what?

2   When Harry Truman learned of the success of the Manhattan Project, he knew he was faced with a decision of unprecedented gravity. The capacity to end the war with Japan was in his hands, but it would involve unleashing the most terrible weapon ever known.

3   American soldiers and civilians were weary from four years of war, yet the Japanese military was refusing to give up their fight. American forces occupied Okinawa and Iwo Jima and were intensely fire bombing Japanese cities. But Japan had an army of 2 million strong stationed in the home islands guarding against invasion.

4   For Truman, the choice whether or not to use the atomic bomb was the most difficult decision of his life.

5   First, an Allied demand for an immediate unconditional surrender was made to the leadership in Japan. Although the demand stated that refusal would result in total destruction, no mention of any new weapons of mass destruction was made. The Japanese military command rejected the request for unconditional surrender, but there were indications that a conditional surrender was possible.

6   Regardless, on August 6, 1945, a plane called the Enola Gay dropped an atomic bomb on the city of Hiroshima. Instantly, 70,000 Japanese citizens were vaporized. In the months and years that followed, an additional 100,000 perished from burns and radiation sickness.

7   Two days later, the Soviet Union declared war on Japan. On August 9, a second atomic bomb was dropped on Nagasaki, where 80,000 Japanese people perished.

8   On August 14, 1945, the Japanese surrendered. Critics have charged that Truman's decision was a barbaric act that brought negative long-term consequences to the United States. A new age of nuclear terror led to a dangerous arms race.

9   Some military analysts insist that Japan was on its knees and the bombings were simply unnecessary. The American government was accused of racism on the grounds that such a device would never have been used against white civilians.

10   Other critics argued that American diplomats had ulterior motives. The Soviet Union had entered the war against Japan, and the atomic bomb could be read as a strong message for the Soviets to tread lightly. In this respect, Hiroshima and Nagasaki may have been the first shots of the Cold War as well as the final shots of World War II. Regardless, the United States remains the only nation in the world to have used a nuclear weapon on another nation.

11   Truman stated that his decision to drop the bomb was purely military. A Normandy-type amphibious landing would have cost an estimated million casualties. Truman believed that the bombs saved Japanese lives as well. Prolonging the war was not an option for the President. Over 3,500 Japanese kamikaze raids had already wrought great destruction and loss of American lives.

12   The President rejected a demonstration of the atomic bomb to the Japanese leadership. He knew there was no guarantee the Japanese would surrender if the test succeeded, and he felt that a failed demonstration would be worse than none at all. Even the scientific community failed to foresee the awful effects of radiation sickness. Truman saw little difference between atomic bombing Hiroshima and fire bombing Dresden or Tokyo.

13   The ethical debate over the decision to drop the atomic bomb will never be resolved. The bombs did, however, bring an end to the most destructive war in history. The Manhattan Project that produced it demonstrated the possibility of how a nation's resources could be mobilized.

14   Pandora's box was now open. The question that came flying out was, "How will the world use its nuclear capability?" It is a question still being addressed on a daily basis.

8. Which detail from the text best supports the idea that the destructive effects of the atomic bomb were felt long after the bomb was dropped?
   (A) "For Truman, the choice whether or not to use the atomic bomb was the most difficult decision of his life."
   (B) "In the months and years that followed, an additional 100,000 perished from burns and radiation sickness."
   (C) "A new age of nuclear terror led to a dangerous arms race."
   (D) "Over 3,500 Japanese kamikaze raids had already wrought great destruction and loss of American lives."

9. Which of the following is the main idea of the passage?
   (A) The atomic bomb was one of many factors that helped to end World War II.
   (B) The nuclear bombing of Hiroshima was the result of a race between the United States and Russia to prove their dominance.
   (C) Though the dropping of the atomic bomb on Hiroshima helped to end World War II, many people throughout history, including Truman himself, struggle with whether or not it was right.
   (D) Dropping the atomic bomb was the only way to end World War II.

10. What effect did dropping the atomic bomb on Hiroshima NOT have?

 Ⓐ 70,000 Japanese citizens were killed.

 Ⓑ The Soviet Union declared war on the United States.

 Ⓒ 100,000 survivors of the atomic bomb later died of burns and radiation sickness.

 Ⓓ It was a factor that led to Japan surrendering to the United States.

11. Which word(s) help you to understand the meaning of the word barbaric in Paragraph 8?

 Ⓐ surrendered

 Ⓑ critics

 Ⓒ negative

 Ⓓ decision

12. How is the text in Paragraph 6 arranged?

 Ⓐ problem and solution

 Ⓑ cause and effect

 Ⓒ compare and contrast

 Ⓓ description

13. What can the reader infer about the author's opinion of the atomic bomb?

 Ⓐ the author is fascinated about the bomb

 Ⓑ the author is regretful about the bomb

 Ⓒ the author is angry about the bomb

 Ⓓ the author is questioning about the bomb

14. Which of the following best reflects the author's message?

 Ⓐ Dropping the atomic bomb on Hiroshima was a difficult decision, but one that was made to help end a destructive war.

 Ⓑ President Truman was in full support of ending the war through nuclear weapons.

 Ⓒ The United States' decision to drop the atomic bomb can largely be blamed on Russia.

 Ⓓ The devastating effects of dropping the atomic bomb on Hiroshima were felt throughout Japan.

Passage 3: Living in the Information Age
by USHistory.org

1   Some have begun to call it the Information Revolution. Technological changes brought dramatic new options to Americans living in the 1990s. From the beginning of the decade until the end, new forms of entertainment, commerce, research, work, and communication became commonplace in the United States. The driving force behind much of this change was an innovation popularly known as the Internet.

2   Personal computers had become widespread by the end of the 1980s. Also available was the ability to connect these computers over local or even national networks. Through a device called a modem, individual users could link their computer to a wealth of information using conventional phone lines. What lay beyond the individual computer was a vast domain of information known as cyberspace.

3   Upon its release in 1983 the Apple "Lisa" computer — named for one of its developers daughters — was supposed to revolutionize personal computing. But interest in "Lisa" was minimal due to its nearly $10,000 price tag and the introduction of the much more affordable "Macintosh" a year later.

4   The Internet was developed during the 1970s by the Department of Defense. In the case of an attack, military advisers suggested the advantage of being able to operate one computer from another terminal. In the early days, the Internet was used mainly by scientists to communicate with other scientists. The Internet remained under government control until 1984.

5   One early problem faced by Internet users was speed. Phone lines could only transmit information at a limited rate. The development of fiber-optic cables allowed for billions of bits of information to be received every minute. Companies like Intel developed faster microprocessors, so personal computers could process the incoming signals at a more rapid rate.

6   In the early 1990s, the World Wide Web was developed, in large part, for commercial purposes. Corporations created home pages where they could place text and graphics to sell products. Soon airline tickets, hotel reservations, books, and even cars and homes could be purchased online. Colleges and universities posted research data on the Internet, so students could find valuable information without leaving their dormitories. Companies soon discovered that work could be done at home and submitted online, so a whole new class of telecommuters began to earn a living from home offices unshaven and wearing pajamas.

7   New forms of communication were introduced. Electronic mail, or email, was a convenient way to send a message to associates or friends. Messages could be sent and received at the

convenience of the individual. A letter that took several days to arrive could be read in minutes. Internet service providers like America Online and CompuServe set up electronic chat rooms. These were open areas of cyberspace where interested parties could join in a conversation with perfect strangers.

8   Advocates of the Internet cited its many advantages. The commercial possibilities were limitless. Convenience was greatly improved. Chat rooms and email allowed individuals to converse who may never have had the opportunity in the past. Educational opportunities were greatly enhanced because of the wealth of knowledge now placed at the fingertips of any wired individual. "Surfing the 'net" became a pastime in and of itself.

9   Critics charged that the Internet created a technological divide that increased the gap between the haves and have-nots. Those who could not afford a computer or a monthly access fee were denied these possibilities. Many decried the impersonal nature of electronic communication compared to a telephone call or a handwritten letter. Hate groups were using the Internet to expand their bases and recruit new members. The unregulated nature of the Internet allowed inappropriate content to be broadcast to millions of homes. Protecting children from these influences, or even from meeting violent predators would prove to be difficult.

10   Regardless of its drawbacks, by the end of the 1990s, the world was fast becoming wired.

15. What does the author mean when he says, "Critics charged that the Internet created a technological divide that increased the gap between the haves and have-nots"?
    - (A) Instead of creating more connection between people, critics believed the Internet actually divided people because of their differing opinions.
    - (B) Critics believed the Internet would prevent further technological advances.
    - (C) Contrary to the belief that the Internet would give all people more opportunities, critics argued that it actually created a divide between those who could afford to have it and those who couldn't.
    - (D) The Internet was a source of frustration for both those who could afford it and those who couldn't.

16. Which of the following sentences best reflects the main idea of paragraph 5?
    - (A) "One early problem faced by Internet users was speed."
    - (B) "Phone lines could only transmit information at a limited rate."
    - (C) "The development of fiber-optic cables allowed for billions of bits of information to be received every minute."
    - (D) "Companies like Intel developed faster microprocessors, so personal computers could process the incoming signals at a more rapid rate."

17. What effect did the lack of regulation on the Internet have on its early users?
    (A) People who couldn't afford to have the Internet didn't have access.
    (B) Businesses were able to sell products and services over the Internet.
    (C) People across the world were able to communicate long distance.
    (D) People, including children, were exposed to dangerous content on the Internet.

18. Which of the following synonyms could be a replacement for the word *advocate* in Paragraph 8?
    (A) lawyer
    (B) recommend
    (C) supporter
    (D) adviser

19. How is the information in Paragraphs 8 and 9 arranged?
    (A) chronological
    (B) cause and effect
    (C) compare and contrast
    (D) sequential

20. What can the reader infer about how the author feels about the subject of the passage?
    (A) The author is a critic of the Internet and its dangers.
    (B) The author is an advocate for the Internet and its many uses.
    (C) The author writes as an objective observer, not including personal feelings.
    (D) The author feels the benefits provided by the Internet outweigh the disadvantages.

21. Which of the following best reflects the author's message?
    (A) The Internet changed the way people live and interact in the 1990s.
    (B) The Internet brought about many drastic changes that have negatively impacted people.
    (C) Personal computers changed the way people live in the 1980s and 90s.
    (D) The Internet brought about many conveniences for everyone.

Passage 4: Visiting Grandfather

1   The sky was still dark when I woke up on the morning my family was supposed to go on vacation to the lake near my grandparents' house. I tried to go back to sleep, but I was too excited, so I ran into my parents' bedroom.

2   My dad wasn't too happy that I was waking them up so early. "It's five in the morning," he whispered. "Go back to sleep."

3   "I can't," I replied. "My mind won't be quiet."

4   My dad groaned and got up out of bed. "Come on, Kiddo," he said and led me to the kitchen. He poured me a bowl of cereal and sat down at the table across from me while I ate.

5   "Listen," my dad said. "I know you're excited about the trip, but you have to keep in mind that this year is going to be a little different."

6   "I know," I said between bites. My grandfather, the strongest man I've ever known, was recently diagnosed with cancer. Usually, summer trips consisted of us riding out on the boat on the open water with grandfather behind the wheel. This year, each day would be up to how he felt, which, according to my mother, wasn't very good most days.

7   "It might not be as fun this time," my dad said. "And we can't complain. Your grandfather has helped us out a lot over the years."

8   My dad didn't realize how close my grandfather and I were, I guess. Sure, boating is fun, but it wouldn't be the same without grandfather. Going out on the boat wasn't what had me up so early.

9   "I'll have fun," I finally said after finishing my last bite. "I always have fun."

10   My dad shrugged his shoulders and stood up. "Let's try to get some more sleep, okay?"

11   I shook my head. I knew I wouldn't be able to go back to sleep, but I could let my parents sleep a little while longer.

12   I walked back to my room and got back into bed, thinking about all the ways grandfather and I could have fun without going anywhere. The list was longer than I thought.

22. Which quote from the text best supports the idea that the narrator cares more about the time he can spend with his grandfather than the fun things his grandfather can provide?

 Ⓐ "The sky was still dark when I woke up on the morning my family was supposed to go on vacation to the lake near my grandparents' house."

 Ⓑ "I know you're excited about the trip, but you have to keep in mind that this year is going to be a little different."

 Ⓒ "Sure, boating is fun, but it wouldn't be the same without grandfather."

 Ⓓ "I knew I wouldn't be able to go back to sleep, but I could let my parents sleep a little while longer."

23. Which of the following best reflects the theme of the passage?

 Ⓐ Tragedy can strike at any moment.

 Ⓑ Relationships are what make life worth living.

 Ⓒ A good night's sleep is important before a long trip.

 Ⓓ Change is a natural part of life.

24. What can the reader NOT infer about the narrator's father?

 Ⓐ He's resentful of his son's relationship with his grandfather.

 Ⓑ He's compassionate toward his son.

 Ⓒ He's not accustomed to waking up early.

 Ⓓ He greatly respects the narrator's grandfather.

25. Which of the following is the best synonym for the words *consisted of* in Paragraph 6?

 Ⓐ existed

 Ⓑ included

 Ⓒ embraced

 Ⓓ incorporated

26. The author includes the information in Paragraph 6 most likely to

 Ⓐ show that the narrator didn't care about how the trip would be different.

 Ⓑ give the narrator a reason to go back to sleep.

 Ⓒ help the reader understand why the trip would be different.

 Ⓓ describe how the narrator planned to spend his summer.

27. From what point-of-view is the story told?

 Ⓐ first person

 Ⓑ second person

 Ⓒ third person objective

 Ⓓ third person omniscient

28. If the author were to include an image next to Paragraph 12, which of the following image descriptions would best fit?

    (A) a boat on a lake

    (B) a boy and his grandfather riding bikes

    (C) a boy and his grandfather playing checkers

    (D) a boy and his grandfather shopping

Directions: Read this passage. Then answer questions through 29-35.

Passage 5: The Peanut Man
by America's Library

1   George Washington Carver was always interested in plants. When he was a child, he was known as the "plant doctor." He had a secret garden where he grew all kinds of plants. People would ask him for advice when they had sick plants. Sometimes he'd take their plants to his garden and nurse them back to health.

2   Later, when he was teaching at Tuskegee Institute, he put his plant skills to good use. Many people in the South had been growing only cotton on their land. Cotton plants use most of the nutrients in the soil. (Nutrients provide nourishment to plants.) So the soil becomes "worn out" after a few years. Eventually, cotton will no longer grow on this land.

3   This was especially bad for poor African American farmers, who relied on selling cotton to support themselves. Carver was dedicated to helping those farmers, so he came up with a plan.

4   Carver knew that certain plants put nutrients back into the soil. One of those plants is the peanut! Peanuts are also a source of protein.

5   Carver thought that if those farmers planted peanuts, the plants would help restore their soil, provide food for their animals, and provide protein for their families--quite a plant! In 1896 peanuts were not even recognized as a crop in the United States, but Carver would help change that.

6   Carver told farmers to rotate their crops: plant cotton one year, then the next year plant peanuts and other soil-restoring plants, like peas and sweet potatoes. It worked! The peanut plants grew and produced lots of peanuts. The plants added enough nutrients to the soil so cotton grew the next year. Now the farmers had lots of peanuts--too many for their families and animals--and no place to sell the extras. Again, Carver had a plan. Do you know what he did?

7   Carver invented all kinds of things made out of peanuts. He wrote down more than 300 uses for peanuts, including peanut milk, peanut paper, and peanut soap. Carver thought

that if farmers started making things out of peanuts, they'd have to buy fewer things and would be more self-sufficient. And if other people started making things out of peanuts, they would want to buy the extra peanuts, so the farmers would make more money. Although not many of Carver's peanut products were ever mass-produced, he did help spread the word about peanuts.

8   Peanuts became more and more popular. By 1920 there were enough peanut farmers to form the United Peanut Association of America (UPAA). In 1921 the UPAA asked Carver to speak to the U.S. Congress about the many uses for peanuts. Soon the whole country had heard of George Washington Carver, the Peanut Man! And by 1940 peanuts had become one of the top six crops in the U.S.

29. Which detail from the text best supports the idea that Carver was concerned about the welfare of others?
   (A) "George Washington Carver was always interested in plants."
   (B) "Carver knew that certain plants put nutrients back into the soil."
   (C) "Carver thought that if those farmers planted peanuts, the plants would help restore their soil, provide food for their animals, and provide protein for their families — quite a plant!"
   (D) "Carver invented all kinds of things made out of peanuts."

30. Which of the following is the main idea of paragraph 2?
   (A) Carter put his knowledge of plants to good use as a teacher at Tuskegee Institute.
   (B) Cotton was the primary crop of farmers in the South.
   (C) Crops need soil rich in nutrients.
   (D) Growing cotton year after year can wear out the nutrients of soil, making it unusable.

31. What effect did Carver's "more than 300 uses for peanuts" have on farmers?
   (A) Word spread about peanuts, causing more and more farmers to become peanut farmers.
   (B) Peanut products, such as peanut milk and peanut soap, were mostly ignored by farmers.
   (C) Farmers were able to replace the majority of their common household products with products made from peanuts.
   (D) Peanuts grew out of popularity, forcing farmers to return to cotton as their primary crop.

32. Which of the following synonyms best fits the context of the word *restore* in Paragraph 5?

    (A) replace

    (B) update

    (C) rehabilitate

    (D) remit

33. How is the text in Paragraph 6 arranged?

    (A) chronological

    (B) cause and effect

    (C) compare and contrast

    (D) sequential

34. What can the reader infer the author's opinion is of George Washington Carver?

    (A) admiring

    (B) uncaring

    (C) unaffected

    (D) frustrated

35. Which of the following best reflects the author's message?

    (A) George Washington Carver was always interested in plants.

    (B) Farmers in the South were forced to give up planting cotton in favor of peanuts.

    (C) George Washington Carver became known as "the Peanut Man" for his solution to restoring the nutrients in soil affected by cotton farming.

    (D) George Washington Carver was responsible for over 300 uses of peanuts.

NY STATE STANDARDS ASSESSMENT

ELA
Practice Test Two

Session One

Answer Key &
Explanations

1. **D.** Sasha's mother, who obviously knows she took a shortcut to cleaning her room in order to play with her slime, handles the situation not with anger but a question. ""I think it might be time to start taking some breaks from the break, don't you think?" she says, then points out the closet where she stuffed all of her toys. Sasha's reaction is to stop what she's doing and fix the situation because she doesn't want her mom to be disappointed. The reader knows that Sasha is motivated by love and not fear when she chooses later on to spend time with her mom instead of playing with her slime. **Standard RL.5.1**

2. **B.** Answer A is a negative lesson to learn from a story and not one the author seems to condone. Instead, the author seems to be showing the importance of being responsible as well as spending time with the people we love over focusing exclusively on our own entertainment. **Standard RL.5.2**

3. **D.** Since there's no indication that her mother was mad or took her privileges away, contrary to what she thought would happen, Sasha's relationship with her mother seems to be a good one. She wants to do what is right because her mother has taught her that doing the right thing is important. **Standard RL.5.3**

4. **B.** In the context of the sentence, it's clear that confiscate means to take away temporarily, in this case as a way to ensure that Sasha does her chores properly. **Standard RL.5.4**

5. **A.** The author includes ther minor detail to give the reader a clue before presenting the problem that Sasha's mother has something to talk to her about. While the other three answers could be correct in a different context, the context of the story emphasizes answer A. **Standard RL.5.5**

6. **D.** The story follows Sasha and her perspective from beginning to end. **Standard RL.5.6**

7. **B.** Answer B captures the main conflict of the story and contrasts with the passage's title in a way that hints at the problem before the reader reads the story. The image of a mother's angry face would not be an accurate reflection of the way the mother felt, as she felt disappointed, not angry. **Standard RL.5.7**

8. **B.** This text reveals that, although the atomic bomb initially killed 70,000 Japanese citizens, the effects of the bomb's fire power and radiation killed many more in the months and years after it was dropped. **Standard RI.5.1**

9. **C.** Answer A is incorrect because the focus isn't on the atomic bomb among other factors helping to end the war. Answer B is incorrect because the nuclear arms race began after the U.S. dropped the bomb on Hiroshima. As the title of the passage indicates, Answer C is correct because the bomb did help end the war, but whether or not it was right to drop it remains a question, and the decision to drop the bomb was indeed a struggle for President Truman himself. Contrary to Answer D, the passage implies that there might have been other possible ways the war could have ended. **Standard RI.5.2**

10. **B.** All of the answer options with the exception of B were mentioned as effects of the U.S. dropping the atomic bomb on Hiroshima. **Standard RI.5.3**

11. **C.** In the context of the sentence, it's clear that barbaric has a negative connotation. The other options don't aid the reader in guessing what barbaric means. **Standard RI.5.4**

12. **B.** Paragraph 6 describes the event of the U.S. dropping the bomb on Hiroshima (the cause) before describing its effects (70,000 then 100,000 killed). **Standard RI.5.5**

13. **D.** It's clear throughout the passage that the author is questioning the rightness of the U.S. dropping the bomb on Hiroshima. **Standard RI.5.6**

14. **A.** Answer A succinctly summarizes the author's argument throughout the passage. Answer D could be true, but the author does not focus on this issue. Answers B and C are not supported by the text. **Standard RI.5.8**

15. **C.** The author uses the phrase "haves and have nots" as a description of people who are wealthy and people who are poor, so the phrase is used to describe a technological divide between those groups of people. Answer A may act as a distractor because it also describes a divide between groups of people, but the divide is caused by differing opinions. **Standard RI.5.1**

16. **A.** As the first sentence of the paragraph, Answer A is acting as the topic sentence. All the other answer choices are supporting details in the paragraph. **Standard RI.5.2**

17. **D.** According to Paragraph 9, because the Internet was unregulated, people were exposed to and sharing inappropriate content over the Internet. **Standard RI.5.3**

18. **C.** In the context of the sentence, it's clear that the author is describing supporters of the Internet, whereas the other answer choices don't fit the context. **Standard RI.5.4**

19. **C.** The author spends a paragraph focused on advocates of the Internet and another paragraph focused on critics of the Internet, setting up the structure of compare and contrast. **Standard RI.5.5**

20. **C.** The author communicates the information about early Internet in an objective way, without including personal feelings about the subject. **Standard RI.5.6**

21. **A.** Answer A is correct because it captures the overall idea of the text. Answer B only covers one aspect of how the Internet has affected people. Answer C may act as a distractor because the beginning of the passage discusses personal computers. Answer D is incorrect because the article mentions that the conveniences brought about by the Internet were not accessible to everyone because some people were too poor to have the Internet. **Standard RI.5.8**

22. **C.** In this option, as opposed to the others, the narrator is considering the fun time he always has with his grandfather on the lake, but states that it wouldn't be as fun if his grandfather was not there. The presence of his grandfather is the determining factor of whether or not something is fun, not whether the grandfather is actively doing something in particular with the narrator. **Standard RL.5.1**

23. **B.** While Answers A and D are certainly true in the type of situation the story describes, the context of the story emphasizes the boy's relationship with his grandfather and how important and influential it is to him. **Standard RL.5.2**

24. **A.** While the father doesn't seem to understand the deep closeness of the relationship between the grandfather and the narrator, there's not any indication that the father resents the relationship the son has with the grandfather. All the other answer options are inferences the reader could make about the narrator's father. **Standard RL.5.3**

25. **B.** While all of the words are synonyms, Answer B is the only answer that fits the context and maintains the meaning. **Standard RL.5.4**

26. **C.** While Answer D might be distracting because the paragraph does describe the typical summer vacation for the narrator, the element that is lost without this paragraph is the reason why the summer vacation will be different, which is the grandfather's cancer. **Standard RL.5.5**

27. **A.** The narrator uses first person pronouns throughout. **Standard RL.5.6**

28. **C.** All the other answers require the boy and his grandfather to leave the grandfather's home. Since he's making a list of things he and his grandfather can do without leaving home, Answer C is the only correct one. **Standard RL.5.7**

29. **C.** This text reveals Carver's advice to the farmers, which he gives to help them maintain healthy soil from year to year so that they will be able to continue to support themselves. **Standard RI.5.1**

30. **D.** While all of the other answer choices are details mentioned in Paragraph 2, the author is using Paragraph 2 to describe the problem that Carver would solve, which was the way cotton crops depleted the nutrients of soil from year to year. This depletion would eventually make the soil unusable, costing the farmers their livelihood. **Standard RI.5.2**

31. **A.** While Carver's uses for peanuts never achieved the popularity of other products made from other materials, Carver's work with peanuts caused people to talk about it, and peanuts grew in popularity as a result. Consequently, more farmers saw the potential in providing for their families through peanut farming. **Standard RI.5.3**

32. **C.** In the context of the sentence, it's clear that Carver intended to help the farmers rehabilitate their soil after the soil lost nutrients from growing cotton. Answer A communicates the idea that the farmers would be replacing their soil, which would have been a highly expensive proposition. Answer B, while close to the meaning, implies that there was something inherently missing from the soil, as opposed to being a consequence of growing cotton, that the farmers needed to add to the soil

to keep it working. Answer D communicates the idea of "canceling" the soil, which is obviously incorrect. **Standard RI.5.4**

33. **B.** Paragraph 6 describes what Carver told the farmers to do (the cause) in order to restore nutrients to their soil (the effect). **Standard RI.5.5**

34. **A.** When the author describes Carver as "the Peanut Man," he/she uses an exclamation mark, which communicates excitement about the subject. Furthermore, the author's tone throughout handles the subject with an admiring tone. **Standard RI.5.6**

35. **C.** As the title of the piece reveals, the author's message in this text is building toward the revelation of why George Washington Carver is known as "the Peanut Man." **Standard RI.5.8**

NY STATE STANDARDS ASSESSMENT

ELA
Practice Test Two

Session Two

Directions: Read this passage. Then answer questions through 36-38.

Passage 6: What is the International Space Station
by NASA

1   The International Space Station is a large spacecraft in orbit around Earth. It serves as a home where crews of astronauts and cosmonauts live. The space station is also a unique science laboratory. Several nations worked together to build and use the space station. The space station is made of parts that were assembled in space by astronauts. It orbits Earth at an average altitude of approximately 250 miles. It travels at 17,500 mph. This means it orbits Earth every 90 minutes. NASA is using the space station to learn more about living and working in space. These lessons will make it possible to send humans farther into space than ever before.

2   **How Old Is the Space Station?**
The first piece of the International Space Station was launched in November 1998. A Russian rocket launched the Russian Zarya (zar EE uh) control module. About two weeks later, the space shuttle Endeavour met Zarya in orbit. The space shuttle was carrying the U.S. Unity node. The crew attached the Unity node to Zarya.

3   More pieces were added over the next two years before the station was ready for people to live there. The first crew arrived on November 2, 2000. People have lived on the space station ever since. More pieces have been added over time. NASA and its partners from around the world completed construction of the space station in 2011.

4   **How Big Is the Space Station?**
The space station has the volume of a five-bedroom house or two Boeing 747 jetliners. It is able to support a crew of six people, plus visitors. On Earth, the space station would weigh almost a million pounds. Measured from the edges of its solar arrays, the station covers the area of a football field including the end zones. It includes laboratory modules from the United States, Russia, Japan and Europe.

5   **What Are the Parts of the Space Station?**
In addition to the laboratories where astronauts conduct science research, the space station has many other parts. The first Russian modules included basic systems needed for the space station to function. They also provided living areas for crew members. Modules called "nodes" connect parts of the station to each other.

6   Stretching out to the sides of the space station are the solar arrays. These arrays collect energy from the sun to provide electrical power. The arrays are connected to the station with a long truss. On the truss are radiators that control the space station's temperature.

7   Robotic arms are mounted outside the space station. The robot arms were used to help

build the space station. Those arms also can move astronauts around when they go on spacewalks outside. Other arms operate science experiments.

8   Astronauts can go on spacewalks through airlocks that open to the outside. Docking ports allow other spacecraft to connect to the space station. New crews and visitors arrive through the ports. Astronauts fly to the space station on the Russian Soyuz. Robotic spacecraft use the docking ports to deliver supplies.

9   Why Is the Space Station Important?

The space station has made it possible for people to have an ongoing presence in space. Human beings have been living in space every day since the first crew arrived. The space station's laboratories allow crew members to do research that could not be done anywhere else. This scientific research benefits people on Earth. Space research is even used in everyday life. The results are products called "spinoffs." Scientists also study what happens to the body when people live in microgravity for a long time. NASA and its partners have learned how to keep a spacecraft working well. All of these lessons will be important for future space exploration.

10   NASA currently is working on a plan to explore other worlds. The space station is one of the first steps. NASA will use lessons learned on the space station to prepare for human missions that reach farther into space than ever before.

36. What details does the author include to support the idea that collaboration is an important part of the International Space Station? Use details from the passage to support your answer.

_____

_____

_____

_____

_____

_____

_____

_____

_____

_____

_____

37. What two important functions does the International Space Station serve, according to the author? Use details from the passage to support your answer.

_____

_____

_____

_____

_____

_____

_____

_____

_____

_____

_____

38. How will the International Space Station benefit people in the future? Use details from the passage to support your answer.

_____

_____

_____

_____

_____

_____

_____

_____

_____

_____

_____

_____

Passage 7 : Learning to Read
by Francis Ellen Watkins Harper

[1]   Very soon the Yankee teachers
Came down and set up school;
But, oh! how the Rebs did hate it,—
It was agin' their rule.

[5]   Our masters always tried to hide
Book learning from our eyes*;
Knowledge didn't agree with slavery—
'Twould make us all too wise.
But some of us would try to steal

[10]   A little from the book,
And put the words together,
And learn by hook or crook.
I remember Uncle Caldwell,
Who took pot-liquor fat

[15]   And greased the pages of his book,
And hid it in his hat.
And had his master ever seen
The leaves up on his head,
He'd have thought them greasy papers,

[20]   But nothing to be read.
And there was Mr. Turner's Ben,
Who heard the children spell,
And picked the words right up by heart,
And learned to read 'em well.

[25]   Well, the Northern folks kept sending
The Yankee teachers down;
And they stood right up and helped us,
Though Rebs did sneer and frown.
And, I longed to read my Bible,

[30]   For precious words it said;
      But when I begun to learn it,
      Folks just shook their heads,
      And said there is no use trying,
      Oh! Chloe, you're too late;

[35]   But as I was rising sixty,
      I had no time to wait.
      So I got a pair of glasses,
      And straight to work I went,
      And never stopped till I could read

[40]   The hymns and Testament.
      Then I got a little cabin—
      A place to call my own—
      And I felt as independent
      As the queen upon her throne.

* Slaves were required to have travel passes signed by their masters in order to travel from one place to another. Slave owners feared giving slaves the ability to read and write would allow them to forge these documents and escape to freedom.

39. What challenge does the narrator face when she decides to start reading at an older age? Use details from the passage to support your answer.

_____

_____

_____

_____

_____

_____

_____

_____

_____

_____

_____

_____

40. Why didn't the masters want their slaves learning to read? Use details from the passage to support your answer.

_____

_____

_____

_____

_____

_____

_____

_____

_____

_____

_____

_____

41. Compare the value people place upon literacy in the poem to how literacy is valued today.Use details from the passage to support your answer.

_____

_____

_____

_____

_____

_____

_____

_____

_____

_____

_____

_____

Directions: Read this passage. Then answer question 42.

Passage 8: What is Antarctica
by NASA

1   Antarctica is a continent. It is Earth's fifth largest continent. Antarctica is covered in ice. Antarctica covers Earth's South Pole.

2   **What Is Antarctica Like?**

Antarctica is the coldest place on Earth. The temperature in the winter is cold enough to freeze water all the time. The temperature in the middle of Antarctica is much colder than the temperature on the coasts.

3   Antarctica has two seasons: summer and winter. Earth is tilted in space and the direction of tilt never changes. During summer, Antarctica is on the side of Earth tilted toward the sun. It is always sunny. In winter, Antarctica is on the side of Earth tilted away from the sun. Then, the continent is always dark.

4   Antarctica is a desert. It does not rain or snow a lot there. When it snows, the snow does not melt and builds up over many years to make large, thick sheets of ice, called ice sheets. Antarctica is made up of lots of ice in the form of glaciers, ice shelves and icebergs.

5   Antarctica has no trees or bushes. The only plants that can live in a place that cold are moss and algae.

6.   **Who Lives in Antarctica?**

Antarctica is too cold for people to live there for a long time. Scientists take turns going there to study the ice. Tourists visit Antarctica in the summers. The oceans around Antarctica are home to many types of whales. Antarctica is also home to seals and penguins.

7   **What Can NASA Learn about Earth from Studying Antarctica?**

NASA uses satellites to study Antarctica. NASA wants to know how Antarctica is changing. Scientists want to know what the changes in Earth's climate are doing to Antarctica's ice sheets. They also want to know what changes in Antarctica's ice might do to Earth's climate.

8   One tool that NASA uses is ICESat. That stands for the Ice, Cloud and land Elevation Satellite. Using ICESat, NASA can measure changes in the size of Antarctica's ice sheets. ICESat also helps NASA understand how changing polar ice may affect the rest of the planet. Melting ice sheets in Antarctica may change sea levels all over the world.

9   NASA instruments have also helped scientists create detailed maps of Antarctica. The maps help researchers when planning trips to Antarctica. They also give people a clearer view of the continent.

10   **What Can NASA Learn about Space from Studying Antarctica?**

Antarctica is a good place to find meteorites, or rocks that fall from space to Earth. Scientists find more meteorites in Antarctica than any other place in the world. Meteorites are easier to see on the white ice. Also, meteorites that fall to Antarctica are protected by the ice for a long time.

11   NASA sends teams to Antarctica to learn more about the planet Mars. Antarctica and Mars have a lot in common. Both places are cold. Both places are dry like a desert. NASA tested robots in Antarctica that later landed on Mars.

12   NASA also goes to Antarctica to study astronaut nutrition. Like people that are in Antarctica in the winter, astronauts in space are not in the sunlight. The sun helps the human body make vitamins. Scientists study people that visit Antarctica to learn how to help astronauts in space get enough vitamins.

42. How does the author develop the contrasting idea that Antarctica, though almost uninhabitable due to its extremely cold temperatures, gives scientists many opportunities for learning more about the Earth and the universe? Use details from both texts to support your response.

_____

_____

_____

_____

_____

_____

_____

_____

_____

_____

_____

_____

_____

_____

_____

NY STATE STANDARDS ASSESSMENT

ELA
Practice Test Two

Session Two

Answer Key &
Explanations

36. Answers will vary. The text explains that the space station was not the effort of one individual nation, such as the United States. Instead, the author says that "several nations worked together to build and use the space station." Furthermore, the station "includes laboratory modules from the United States, Russia, Japan and Europe." This shows that the space station was a collaborative effort among several nations. Standard RI.5.2

37. Answers will vary. The text describes the two primary functions of the space station as a research laboratory and a home for astronauts conducting that research. The station is "able to support a crew of six people, plus visitors." Because the research being done is in space, the space station's laboratories "allow crew members to do research that could not be done anywhere else." Being able to live on the space, crew members are able to single-mindedly focus on their research and discover more about how humanity could live in space. **Standard RI.5.1**

38. Answers will vary. The text says that "NASA is using the space station to learn more about living and working in space." The reason is so that it will be "possible to send humans farther into space than ever before." Ultimately, NASA hopes to send astronauts into space to explore other worlds, and the space station's research will help them achieve this. **Standard RI.5.8**

39. Answers will vary. The text explains that the narrator, whose name is Chloe, "longed to read [her] Bible." People in her life, however, discouraged her from learning to read because they thought she was too old. Instead of letting other people discourage her, she pushed herself even more. She "got a pair of glasses" and taught herself to read until she could read the Bible for herself. **Standard RL.5.2**

40. Answers will vary. The text explains that the slave owners and people who supported slavery hated the idea of people from the north ("the Yankees") teaching slaves how to read. They believed that slaves gaining literacy "ag[ed] their rule," meaning that their time of being a master of their slave was limited by the slave's literacy. As the note to the poem indicates, the reason for this fear was because the slave owners "feared giving slaves the ability to read and write would allow them to forge [travel passes signed by their masters] and escape to freedom. **Standard RL.5.1**

41. Answers will vary. The text describes the ability to read as something highly valued by people in slavery. They value it so much that they sneak around to get material to read and to teach themselves to read. The narrator gives examples of these types of people who highly value literacy. For example, she describes "Uncle Caldwell, Who took pot-liquor fat And greased the pages of his book, And hid it in his hat" so that no one would realize that he had reading material. It simply looked like greased papers. **Standard RL.5.9**

42. Answers will vary. Example student response: Though the text describes Antarctica as a barren desert with temperatures too cold for human being to live there for long, the author also describes the ways NASA uses Antarctica to make important discoveries about our world and the other worlds surrounding us. One of these ways includes studying Antarctica in order to understand potential climate change on Earth and how rapidly it could spread to other parts of the world.

Additionally, scientists study Antarctica because it's similar in makeup to the planet Mars. Sending a group of individuals to inhabit Mars for a short period of time allows these scientists to study the nutritional habits of the people in those conditions, which will be beneficial as NASA moves forward to explore new areas of space. **Standard RL.5.2**

Made in United States
North Haven, CT
10 September 2024

57196746R00109